AMABEL WILLIAMS-ELLIS & WILLIAM STOBBS

GEORGIAN ENGLAND

Life in England 4

BLACKIE LONDON & GLASGOW

Blackie & Son Limited,
5 Fitzhardinge Street,
London, W.1.
Bishopbriggs, Glasgow.
Blackie & Son (India) Limited, Bombay.

Reproduced and printed in Great Britain by
Colour Reproductions Limited,
Billericay,
Essex.

Limp Edition 216.89005.5
Hard-cased Edition 216.87196.4

ACKNOWLEDGEMENTS

Acknowledgement is due to the following for permission to reproduce illustrations:

THE TRUSTEES OF THE BRITISH MUSEUM, The Press Gang, page 98; Gin Lane, page 100.

THE FITZWILLIAM MUSEUM, Hogarth's The Bench, page 120.

E. L. GREEN-ARMYTAGE, photographs of the Royal Crescent, Bath, pages 122–3.

JARROLD & SONS LIMITED, Wax effigy of Admiral Nelson, page 119.

THE MANSELL COLLECTION, School, page 120; Roundabout, page 125.

THE NATIONAL GALLERY, Hogarth's The Shrimp Girl, page 99; Hogarth's Marriage à la mode, page 100; Gainsborough's Mrs. Siddons, page 107; Stubbs' Lady and Gentleman in a Phaeton, page 121; Goya's Duke of Wellington, page 127.

PHOTO RESEARCHERS, Giant clam and coral on Great Barrier Reef, page 109, photo Graham Pizzey.

By courtesy of the TRUSTEES OF THE NATIONAL MARITIME MUSEUM, GREENWICH, John Harrison's first Marine Timekeeper, page 115.

THE NATIONAL PORTRAIT GALLERY, LONDON, George I, George II, George III, George IV, all page 97; Lady Mary Wortley-Montagu, page 102 ; Fanny Burney, Garrick, both page 107; Faraday, page 114; Byron, Shelley, Wordsworth, all page 124.

REPRODUCED BY GRACIOUS PERMISSION OF HER MAJESTY THE QUEEN, Morier's Culloden, page 103. Copyright Reserved.

THE ROYAL INSTITUTION, page 117, photograph based on a water-colour by Thomas Hosmer Shepherd.

CROWN COPYRIGHT, SCIENCE MUSEUM, LONDON, Stern of 70-gun ship, page 99; bows of 50-gun ship, page 101; Tull's seed-drill, page 104; Newcomen's engine, Arkwright's spinning-machine, both page 114; Trevithick's locomotive, Watt's steam-engine, both page 125; Puffing Billy, Hargreaves' spinning-jenny, both page 126.

THE TATE GALLERY, LONDON, Stanfield's Battle of Trafalgar, page 119, photo John Webb.

THE VICTORIA AND ALBERT MUSEUM, English Family at Tea, page 98; Console Table, Panelled Room, Kent's mirror, all page 102; The Music Room, Porcelain shepherd and shepherdess, both page 106; Chess game, Indian soldiers, both page 112; Old East India Wharf, page 121, photo Art-Wood Photography.

WALTON PHOTOGRAPHIC SUPPLIES, Nelson's Column, page 128.

WEDGWOOD, Plaques, pages 111 and 115.

COLONIAL WILLIAMSBURG, page 110.

WOODMANSTERNE LIMITED, Senior Gatekeeper the Bank of England, photo Howard C. Moore, Coronation Coach, both page 128.

BOOK LIST

THE EXPANSION OF EUROPE IN THE 18TH CENTURY by G. Williams (Blandford 1966). Excellent source book (see author's foreword).

LETTRES PHILOSOPHIQUES by Voltaire, edited by F. A. Taylor (Blackwell). There are English translations.

LADY MARY WORTLEY-MONTAGU by Iris Barry (Benn, 1928). Pleasant biography of an extraordinary woman.

PRINCE CHARLIE IN SONG by Sir Harold Boulton (Bles, 1933). Many less known ballads.

MAN AND THE GOOD EARTH (Blackie, 1958) Junior 'reader' on science in agriculture; GOOD CITIZENS (Bodley Head, 1938). Short lives of Mrs. Siddons, Wren, Halley, etc; CHANGING THE WORLD (Bodley Head, 1936). Short lives of Benjamin Franklin, etc. All by Amabel Williams-Ellis.

THE PLEASURES OF ARCHITECTURE by Clough & Amabel Williams-Ellis (Jonathan Cape, 1924). Buildings and their builders.

THE LIFE OF SAMUEL JOHNSON by James Boswell ('Everyman', 1961).

THE COURT AT WINDSOR by C. Hibbert (Penguin, 1964). Enlightening gossip: William the Conqueror to Victoria and on.

SOCIAL CONDITIONS IN ENGLAND, 1760–1830, by J. Doncaster (Longmans, 1964). Evidence in pictures.

ENGLISH GIRLHOOD AT SCHOOL by D. Gardiner (O.U.P., 1929). Material otherwise hard to find.

A PICTURE SOURCE BOOK FOR SOCIAL HISTORY, 18TH CENTURY, A PICTURE SOURCE BOOK FOR SOCIAL HISTORY, 19TH CENTURY both by Molly Harrison and A. A. M. Wells (Allen & Unwin, 1955). Small books with well chosen examples.

THE ANCIEN REGIME by C. B. A. Behrens (Thames & Hudson, 1967). Paperback. Very good for French background.

'SIR', SAID DR. JOHNSON by H. C. Biron (Duckworth, 1911). See 'Texts & Comments' ref. page 107. Most amusing.

SIR JOSEPH BANKS by H. C. Cameron (Angus and Robertson, 1966). Biography of a fascinating character.

BEAU NASH by W. Connely (Werner Laurie, 1956). Amusing.

ESSAYS and THE OPIUM EATER by de Quincey. Many popular editions.

SILAS MARNER by George Eliot, published 1861 (Oxford World Classics). First-rate novel for social conditions.

THE FLOATING REPUBLIC by G. E. Manwaring and B. Dobree (Cass, 1966). Important. See 'Texts & Comments' ref. page 117.

MOVEABLE FEASTS by A. Palmer (O.U.P., 1952). Mealtimes. Amusing.

A HISTORY OF AMERICAN PRIVATEERS by E. S. Maclay (Sampson Low, 1900). Hair-raising!

JOLLY ROGER by P. Pringle (Museum Press, 1953). Pirates.

BRITISH CANALS by Charles Hadfield (David and Charles, 1966). A fascinating story.

REJECTED ADDRESSES by J. & H. Smith (Pickering & Chatto, first published in 1812). Famous and funny.

THE LIFE OF ROBERT OWEN by G. D. H. Cole (Cass, 1965). Standard biography.

SCIENCE SINCE 1500 by H. T. Pledge (H.M.S.O., 1966). Admirable reference book.

OCCUPATIONAL COSTUME IN ENGLAND by P. Cunnington & Lucas (A. & C. Black, 1967). Costume book with a difference.

A HISTORY OF MUSIC IN SOUND by G. Abraham (general editor). These and other records of the period should be available at larger public libraries.

Note also several appropriate JACKDAW collections of reprinted contemporary documents edited by John Langdon-Davies (Cape). NO. 12 THE SLAVE TRADE, NO. 23 WOLFE AT QUEBEC, NO. 35 THE EARLY TRADE UNIONS.

Note: THE DICTIONARY OF NATIONAL BIOGRAPHY (in larger public libraries) is not as formidable as it looks. Many entries, though fairly short, are vivid, entertaining and reliable. Try 'Lady Mary Wortley-Montagu', 'Dr. Johnson', 'General Wolfe' and 'Byron'.

AUTHOR'S FOREWORD

By 1715 men and women in Europe had begun to get used to the idea of how big the world is. The Romans and Greeks had believed that Earth was small and as flat as a tray. Now explorers had proved that it was not like that at all.

Indeed the planet itself seemed to have grown to twice its size, and science seemed to have grown in the same sort of way. So many puzzles, from the circulation of the blood to the orbits of the planets, had been tackled, while now there were new ways of doing such things as building ships and working metals. Europeans, the English among them, had begun using certain of those new inventions to bully, and sometimes to enslave, the inhabitants of whole continents. The countries that have Atlantic ports – Portugal, Spain, France, the Netherlands and Britain – had been the most active. Better ocean-going ships had been built which could be manoeuvred in battle in such a way that their crews could fire the new, more efficient cannon in broadside after broadside. Professor Glyndwr Williams writes:

'Great stretches of territory in the Americas had been explored and colonized, the coasts of Africa had been mapped, regular trade routes had been opened to India, China and the Eastern Seas.'

People from European nations sometimes went voyaging just to explore or to get away from persecution. But trade and glory were the great attractions. Professor Williams quotes an Englishman:

'Trade would render (distant) navigation, which is so strange and consequently so terrible to us, easy and familiar. It would greatly increase our shipping and our seamen, which are the true and natural strength of our country.'

'What comparison,' writes a Frenchman, 'can be made between the execution of a project such as this (for pushing French armies down the Mississippi) and the conquest of some little ravaged province bought at expense a hundred times greater?'

So now, far away in the Tropics or the Arctic, there were constant fights amounting to wars between the different nations of Europe.

Quite different ideas about government, science, and the arts, had grown up in France and Britain, now the chief rivals.

Catholic France, with a strong central government and brilliant court, had flourished. Protestant England had been less successful and our King Charles I and his beautiful French Queen had wanted the kind of government that seemed so splendid in France. Instead they had got a Civil War; after the Parliament-men had won and Oliver Cromwell, the Lord Protector, had died, Charles II had been brought back but with only half his father's power. James II had tried to get back more and had been chased off the throne.

As this part of the tale begins George I was King, but the country was ruled sometimes by one and sometimes by another political party – the Whigs or the Tories – whichever managed to get most votes in Parliament, an arrangement that didn't seem to be working too badly.

But the Kings and Princes on the Continent tried to imitate the brilliance of the French Court. However, even if they laughed at us, some Frenchmen rather admired our unfashionable ways.

So this next part of the story begins with the opinions of a particularly sharp-tongued Frenchman about England and about her science and her everyday doings. This was a young man whose own government didn't at all like the way in which he would keep speaking his mind.

vii

ON BREVITY

'I did not wish to bring the whole wood home, even if I could carry it. Therefore I exhort every one who is able, and has many waggons, to wend his way to the same wood where I cut the props.'

KING ALFRED OF WESSEX A.D. 849-900

'The good effects wrought by Founders of Cities, Lawgivers, Fathers of the People, Extirpers of tyrants, and heroes of that class, extend but over narrow spaces and last but for short times; whereas the work of the Inventor, though a thing of less pomp and show, is felt everywhere and lasts for ever.'

FRANCIS BACON 1561-1626

'What makes a nation happy and keeps it so,
What ruins kingdoms and lays cities flat.'

JOHN MILTON 1608-1674

'Bid Harbours open, public Ways extend,
Bid Temples, worthier of the God, ascend;
Bid the broad Arch the dang'rous Flood contain,
The Mole projected break the roaring Main;
Back to his bounds the subject Sea command,
And roll obedient Rivers thro' the Land:
These Honours Peace to happy Britain brings,
These are Imperial Works, and worthy Kings.'

ALEXANDER POPE 1688-1744

'This vile dirty planet of ours – which o' my conscience, with reverence be it spoken, I take to be made up of the shreds and clippings of the rest; – not but the planet is well enough, provided a man could be born in it to a great title or to a great estate.'

LAURENCE STERNE 1713-1768

'When I landed in London it was Spring'

George I

George II

George III

The Prince Regent, later George IV.

Voltaire at Greenwich, A gentle hill rises green behind the buildings. The tale is in the text.

'When I landed in London it was Spring, the sky was cloudless with a light west wind.' So wrote a French exile, Monsieur Voltaire, a young man who was soon to be famous all over Europe and beyond.

He makes his way to Greenwich. Strolling over the turf and among the trees, he sees that some sort of fete is going on and that a number of young people, both men and girls, are riding and caracoling about on horseback. There are also walkers, among them some charming young ladies in white India-muslin who catch his eye. Many of these girls seem to him pretty and all 'well-made, fine young women'. He is surprised to be told that these people are not aristocrats from the Court, but merchants and their families. Here is Voltaire writing to a friend in France, and it amuses him to make the English out to be as odd as possible. How surprised, he says, posterity will be, to be told 'that an island, whose only produce is a little lead, tin, fullers' earth, and coarse wool', has become so prosperous. Why? Not just commerce, he thinks. 'England is a country where the nobles are great without insolence and without vassals, and where the people share in the government without confusion.' One of the oddities is that, in a noble family, the younger sons have no titles and often become traders and merchants.

'Such a custom particularly shocks the Germans (who are always so puffed up with their own noble Pedigrees). They think it dreadful that the son of a British Peer should be no more than a rich and possibly influential private citizen. In Germany where all the sons inherit their father's title everybody seems to be a Prince. Why, there have often been as many as thirty Highnesses in one place at one time and all belonging to the same family!'

As for France, Voltaire goes on, as well as the Dukes Royal and otherwise, anyone who comes up to Paris from the provinces with a little money seems to become a Marquis at the very least; then he puts on fearful airs, talks about 'a man of my rank', and proceeds snub at everyone 'in trade.' Most ridiculous of all, 'the trader is usually a fool enough to blush at this'.

'Which is most useful to a nation, a lord powder'd in the top of the mode, who knows exactly what o'clock the King rises and goes to bed, or the man who helps forward the nation's commerce? No one is exempted in this country from paying taxes because he is a nobleman.'

Not long before, Sir Isaac Newton (then a very old man) had died. He had been given a great funeral and had been buried in Westminster Abbey. Voltaire's remark on this is famous: 'They buried a professor of mathematics as if he had been a Prince who had done good to his subjects'. Voltaire teasingly tells his French friend that this Monsieur Newton's discoveries have disturbed the whole universe. In Paris, space is apparently full of whirligigs of tenuous matter (this was the idea of Descartes, the famous French astronomer) but nothing of the kind is to be supposed in London.

In England 'Talents are the passport to glory'.
1714–1727

The family takes tea (they would have pronounced it 'tay'). He has taken off his wig and wears a comfortable cap on his shaven head. They drink from small handle-less cups. The spaniel wants cake or sugar.

'The Liberty of the Subject'. The crowd is indignant and the children cry as the Press Gang carries off the poor tailor in Gillray's satirical picture.

'Here space is just space – empty! Then in Paris, when you suppose that the moon will give you a high tide, these gentlemen say that on the contrary it'll be low; in France, the sun doesn't come into this business at all, but in England it seems that it's the sun that makes the difference between spring and neap tides. In France, stars, sun, and everything else, are controlled by a push of which no one knows the reason, but with Monsieur Newton it's all done by a pull – an attraction that no one understands, any better!'

Voltaire would not have been Voltaire if he had just flattered the English. About the Royal Society, for example, he writes tartly:

'Two things, and those the most essential to man, are wanting in the Royal Society of London – rewards and laws. A seat in the Academy of Paris is a small but secure fortune to a Geometrician or a Chemist; but members of the Royal Society are at a continual though small expense.'

He discovered something much worse:

'One day when I had hired a boat on the Thames, one of the boatmen, seeing that I was French, began to boast of the freedom of his country and swore that he would rather be a boatman on the Thames than an Archbishop in France. The next day I saw the same man in prison. His feet were in irons and he was begging, holding out his hand to passers-by. I asked him if he still thought so little of being an archbishop in France?'

What had happened to this unhappy man was only too common. The boatman had been seized by the Press-gang and was to be forced to serve on a man-of-war.

'This man's misfortunes moved me very much, but another Frenchman, who was with me, could not help feeling a malicious pleasure that these English who, kept reproaching us for our lack of freedom, were just as much slaves as we were! But I was miserable for there seemed to be no liberty anywhere.'

Voltaire goes to see all the odd characters that he can find. In France Quakers were outlawed. Voltaire visits an eminent member of the Society of Friends in London. He finds 'a hale, ruddy old man dressed in a plain coat and a beaver hat, the brim of which was horizontal, like those of our clergy.' Voltaire asks him why Quakers and Quakeresses wore a special dress.

'Others,' said the Quaker, 'wear the badges and marks of their several dignities, and we those of Christian humility. We never become soldiers. Our God, who has commanded us to love our enemies, would not permit us to cross the seas, merely because murderers, clothed in scarlet and wearing hats two feet high, enlist citizens by a noise made with two little sticks on an extended ass's skin.'

As the reader may feel critical of many things that were then being done and tolerated by British Governments, it is just as well to remember that to Voltaire of the whiplash tongue we seemed to be particularly decent and civilized people.

Voltaire by the way has nothing to say about the reigning monarch, George I. No wonder. The current Whig notables had been as wily as the coalition of Whigs and Tories who had, earlier, got rid of James II (see page 89).

A German prince had conveniently been available, a man who came from a dynasty of rather particularly uncultured princelings that every English aristocrat felt he could despise.

Yet nobody could say that King George of Hanover was a usurper in England, for he was a descendant of James I. He was in fact ideally suitable, for he was stupid, ate and drank too much, and could talk no English. He soon gave up attending the meetings of his Council; so the Council gradually became more and more like the modern Cabinet, and it was, from this time on, presided over by the leader of the Whigs or of the Tories, whichever had a Parliamentary majority. The Court itself almost ceased to be fashionable, for English ladies declared that the German ladies whom the Hanoverians brought with them were ignorant, coarse and dowdy. Thus it comes about that, for the next fifty years or so, from about 1714 to 1760, home politics, with their incessant tug of war between Whigs and Tories, can almost be disregarded – which is lucky, because at this time particularly interesting things were being done by painters, architects, musicians, satirists, poets, and, above

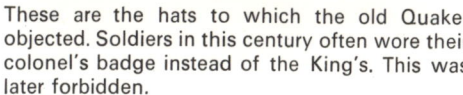
These are the hats to which the old Quaker objected. Soldiers in this century often wore their colonel's badge instead of the King's. This was later forbidden.

all, by scientists, explorers, merchant-adventurers, privateers and pirates.

This was a time when, in science and technics, the great advances that had been made a little earlier were being tried out and applied. It was the practical people (or theoretical men behaving like practical men) who were making the advances.

The case of Edmund Halley is a good sample. Halley was the cheerful son of a soap-boiler and his name is now well known because he had a comet called after him. He realized that it had first been seen at the time of the Norman Conquest and correctly predicted its further returns. As quite a young man he had done notable things (see page 83) for that great man of theory – the mighty, moody Sir Isaac Newton. Young Halley had been given three hundred pounds a year by his father and had sailed in an East Indiaman to St Helena to correct the star-charts of the Southern Hemisphere. He had observed and foretold the movements of both planets and comets, and then he managed to get from the Admiralty command of a small naval vessel (a 'Pink') pleasantly named the *Paramour*. The purpose, as his naval warrant put it, was that of 'visiting His Majesty's

Hogarth's love of life comes out in his famous 'Shrimp Girl'.

The elaborately carved stern of a seventy gun ship

Hogarth satirized the rich. This picture is from a series about a loveless, fashionable marriage. All through this series the debauched young man and the brainless girl are seen as being preyed upon by lawyers, hairdressers, tailors and down-and-out gamblers. They come to a bad end.

Hogarth did not often paint charmingly as in his 'Shrimp girl' page 99. He was a reformer, a satirist, a good hater, in short a brilliant caricaturist. This is low life, his famous 'Gin Lane'. He approved of beer but hated the horrible results of cheap spirits.

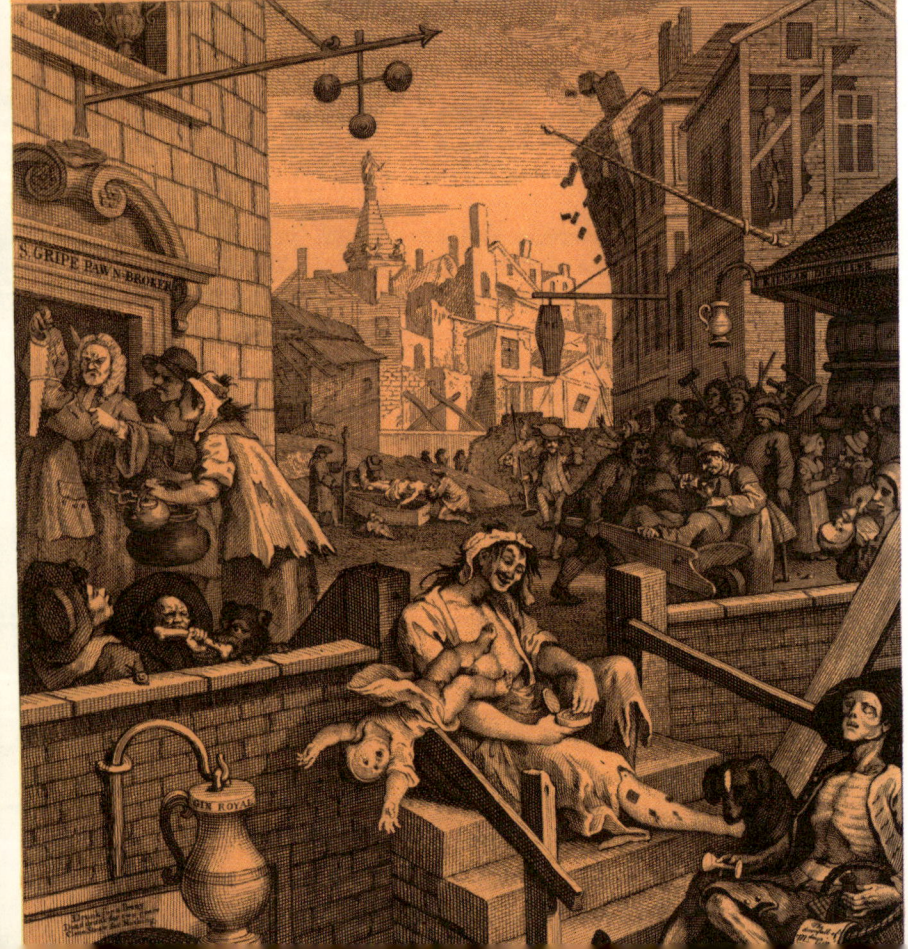

settlements in North America the better to lay down their latitude and longitude'.

Paramour sailed at first in convoy, but when it was time for her to go off on her own, the Second-in-Command flatly refused to sail under this 'Captain Halley', who, he said, 'didn't know enough to command the longboat, let alone the Pink'. Halley proved how wrong this fellow was by himself taking the lieutenant's watches and, a year later, successfully accomplished an audacious voyage South, where he went on charting depths and currents and correcting star-charts till his little *Paramour* met the sullen Antarctic ice and fog.

All this laborious, dangerous, re-making of star-charts was done in the hope of making the long voyages that the merchants demanded less chancy. But the practical men were also tackling something else that had always made navigation dangerous. They were, however, still tackling this danger in an old-fashioned way and not very successfully.

Ships near shore were liable to come to tragic ends. One vicious English inshore hazard, the treacherous Eddystones – rocks off Plymouth Harbour – had already been marked with a lighthouse, but it had been swept away (see page 91). However, for forty-seven years a second lighthouse, also wooden, had stood up to the battering seas and to the merciless chaos of the winds. This second tower had twenty-four candles by way of light. As before, it had been possible only to work at building it on fine days for a couple of hours at each low tide, while with this second Eddystone lighthouse there had been yet another difficulty. We were at war with France, and one day a French privateer took all the builders prisoner. Louis XIV of France, however, sent them back saying that 'though he was at war with England he was not at war with mankind'.

But at last, on a certain dark December night, something disastrous happened. At Trinity House – the body today responsible for the six hundred or more lights round the English coasts – is recorded this extraordinary tale.

'On the night of 2nd December 1755, the

top of the lantern caught fire, probably through a spark from one of the twenty-four candles. The keeper on watch, Harry Hall, was 94 years old. He did his best to put out the fire by throwing water upwards from a bucket. But the leaden roof melted and the molten lead ran down over him, burning him badly: his mouth being open and he looking upwards, some ran down his throat. He called the other keeper, but they could do nothing, the fire being above them all the time. It gradually burnt downwards and finally drove them out on the rock. The fire was seen from the shore and a boat put off which, however, only arrived at ten the next morning. The sea was too rough for the boat to get up to the lighthouse so they threw ropes and dragged the keepers, including poor old Harry Hall, with the lead in his stomach, through the waves to the boat.'

The fire went on burning for five days and the wooden building was entirely destroyed. Harry Hall lived twelve days after he was landed. The Trinity House account goes on:

'The Doctor who attended him made a post-mortem and found a flat oval piece of lead in his stomach which weighed 7 oz. 5 drs. The piece of lead may be seen in the Edinburgh Museum today, how it got there I don't know: it certainly ought to be at Trinity House.'

This second Eddystone lighthouse is a good instance of the kind of progress that was going on. Only a little more practical than the first, it lasted longer, but didn't show any theoretical advance.

Transport was worse, rather than better, for there was a great deal of riding about and above all, every year, more wheeled traffic to churn up the muddy tracks that passed as roads. A few more rivers were being dredged and deepened for more barge traffic and ways of farming were being slowly improved.

The reader is to imagine a countryside in which many of the 'Stately Homes' that are visited today still had the builder's scaffolding round them, and where what are now grassy parks were being laid out and there were only little newly planted trees where now the visitor walks under the shade of tall, leafy chestnut or lime.

Knowledge and practice were at the

The carved and gilded bows of a fifty-gun ship. The bowsprit is cocked up over the lion figure-head.

The dramatic end of the second Eddystone Lighthouse, a better piece of engineering. The difficulty was building on a rock that only showed for two hours at each low tide, while even in good weather, seas burst up on it in raging foam. This wooden lighthouse stood for forty-seven years.

Aristocratic furniture and a lady who used her brains
1718–1745

Lady Mary Wortley-Montagu in Turkish dress with one of her children.

This beautifully carved side-table has a green marble top.

A gilt mirror by William Kent, an architect who was often fortunate in having clients who let him design their furniture as well as their houses.

The furniture and carpet in this panelled room do not look contemporary. Obviously it was not everyone who got rid of everything old when a room was newly done up.

same sort of stage in medicine – there had been some progress, but not much.

Smallpox was now the most dreaded of the infectious diseases. Queen Mary II, wife of William III, had died of it and, though its victims might not always die, they might well be blinded either in one eye or both, and they were often hideously disfigured – with noses out of shape, thickened lips, and loose, leathery, pock-marked skin. A lovely girl or a handsome young man might become horrible to look at after an attack.

It so happened that a certain Lord Edward Wortley-Montagu was sent as ambassador to the Sultan of Turkey and that his wife, Lady Mary Wortley-Montagu – a dashing beauty and a brilliant wit – went with him. She was a fascinating woman (look at her picture alongside) and, being rich and an aristocrat, she got away with being bold and venturesome. 'She neither thinks, speaks, acts or dresses like anybody else,' said a lady who knew her well.

Now in Turkey it had long been the custom for parents to have their children inoculated against smallpox. They dreaded the horrible disfiguring effects of a bad attack of the disease, just as much as the British did, and their rather chancy way of preventing disfigurement, or worse, was deliberately to give their children a mild attack. An old woman would bring infected material in a walnut shell from a patient with a mild form of the disease. The child usually got a mild instead of a violent attack and this almost always prevented a severe attack later. Lady Mary learned about all this and, back in London, she had her own children inoculated. They duly got mild smallpox but were neither blinded nor scarred. Royalty and fashionable parents followed Lady Mary's lead.

This was, like the second Eddystone lighthouse, a first step only.

For over fifty years home politics were, as has been said on page 99, less interesting than science, exploration, or the arts. There were, however, two political events during this time that were both serious and tragic.

The Stuarts, backed by the French,

'Charlie loves good ale and wine'.

twice tried to come back and to take the three kingdoms of England, Scotland and Ireland again. The first attempt, in 1715, was triggered off when the ruling party in England (the Whigs) invited George I to succeed Queen Anne. Anne, James II's daughter, had been tolerable to Scottish people – she was, after all, a Stuart. But not so 'German George'. There was a popular song that began: 'Wha' the deil hae we got for a King, but a wee wee German Lairdie!' and so on for several abusive verses. There was a Highland rising and the Lowland Scots, who agreed with the song, might have rebelled as well, had the Stuart representative (whom the English called 'The Old Pretender', a son of James II) been more attractive and competent. But he was no leader and the Lowland Scots did not rise. Then, for nearly thirty years, while George I and then a second 'wee wee German Lairdie' (George II) reigned, French secret-service men and Scottish and English Jacobites went briskly plotting to and fro across the Channel, but without finding a good opportunity for another try.

At last in 1745, when the English Army was once more fighting on the Continent, an attractive Stuart, Prince Charles Edward, decided to make a gamble of it. 'Sire,' he wrote in a farewell letter to his father, the Old Pretender, 'I go in search of three crowns which I hope to have the honour and happiness of laying at your Majesty's feet. If I fail, your next sight of me shall be in my coffin.'

The rest is what a reader might expect. Most of the Highland Scots did rise; most of the Lowland Scots and the English did not. The Jacobite army marched south and reached Derby. But now the English army was called back from the Continent and the Jacobite army began a long retreat. At Culloden the two armies fought. It is said that after the battle the Highlanders (who had fought exceedingly bravely) were found 'lying dead in layers three or four deep'. The Prince himself escaped and he lived all that summer, in the Western Isles or in the Highlands, hunted by the Redcoats and with a great price on his head.

He was never betrayed. That letter to his father and the many fascinating Jacobite songs and ballads show both Charles Edward's character and the way in which his followers felt about him. A certain Lady Nairne wrote the best known of the ballads almost a generation after the event:

'Speed bonnie boat, like a bird on the wing
'Onward' the sailors cry.
Carry the lad that is born to be King
Over the sea to Skye.'

Another is the song whose first line heads the page.

'Charlie loves good ale and wine,
Charlie loves good brandy,
Charlie loves a pretty lass,
As sweet as sugar candy.'

All have beguiling tunes.

If the pages on agriculture that follow seem a little humdrum after the charm and tragedy of 'the 45', it is good to remember that today Scottish farms in the Lowlands are among the most productive in the world. What came about was in fact a revival in the Lowlands. Scots benefited as much as did the English from what has come to be called 'the Agricultural Revolution', while Edinburgh flourished as never before, becoming one of the European centres of learning and the arts.

The end of 'the Forty-five'. After the Battle of Culloden the Highland dead lay deep on the field. This is after a picture by David Morier who actually drew and interviewed surviving prisoners. The Highlanders are wearing the traditional clan dress – a plaid ten yards long thrown over the shoulder and belted into a kilt.

A 'Jacobite' wine-glass in which to drink to the exiled Stuarts. The rosebud symbolizes the Young Pretender.

'The whole estate farmed in a capital style'.
1750–1800

Fine wheat harvests as well as barley could now be grown on what had once seemed wretchedly bad land. Improvements were devices like better rotation of crops, or clay spread on land that was too light and sandy. Selected seeds could be set in rows by the horse-drill. Such improvements doubled what could be got from arable farms for winter feed for cows.

Model of Jethro Tull's horse-drawn seed-drill. Seed was poured into the wooden hoppers. It dribbled out in two straight rows. Later in the season weeds could be got rid of by hoeing between the rows.

Rather in the same sort of spirit that the first and second Eddystone light-houses were built and protection was attempted against smallpox, so now practical people had begun vigorously, but mostly by rule of thumb, to make real improvements in farming. Even in the country many children had suffered from diseases such as rickets and scurvy, for there was never any fresh milk, butter, or fresh meat all winter and hardly any vegetables. Here and there improvements had been made on some farms (Jethro Tull's for instance) and a little later a certain Arthur Young (see page 106) and a few other go-aheads, came to the conclusion that their forefathers' ways of growing crops (such as leaving each field fallow once in every three years, or the sowing broadcast of poor quality-seed) wasted 'time, seed, land and labour'.

Then noblemen, big squires and writers, began to take up the idea. When Lord Townshend quarrelled with the Prime Minister and resigned from office, he began to experiment on his estates. A wit said that this was ridiculous because these estates were in Norfolk, the county 'where two rabbits fight for one blade of grass!' As for ploughing there, the idea was absurd! 'All you want on that light land is a couple of those same rabbits harnessed to a pocket-knife!'

Lord Townshend was, however, determined to grow turnips and clover. The cows needed roots and clover-hay to eat if they were to stay in milk in the winter. He tried to persuade his tenants, and even ordered them, to sow turnips and to plough deeper. They objected.

He also tried to get them to use Jethro Tull's horse-drill (like the one in the picture). The drill saved time and also seed, which was important if 'selected' seed was being used. It meant too that the seeds could be set in a row. Then, when the cereal crop or the turnips came up, they could be kept free from weeds by hoeing. The tenants objected.

But soon the farms where turnips were grown began to thrive. When she got roots, and clover-hay or lucerne as feed, a good cow could be milked at Christmas. As the reader can guess, improvement

'Tis all hat-barley since the horse-drill came'.

took a long time. But luckily reforms as well as being resisted, can be catching. Another go-ahead Norfolk landowner, Thomas Coke, had taken up the new ideas and declared that quite a lot of other crops not locally grown – such as wheat and kale – could thrive, especially if a better 'rotation' of crops was used.

Squire Coke also – with the usual difficulty – persuaded his tenants to use the horse-drill. More particularly he studied what a sheep-breeder named Bakewell was doing about farm animals.

There were sheep that would neither grow wool nor fatten, also long-legged pigs whose ribs, however much they ate, stuck out like hay-racks, and cattle and horses that were poor milkers or workers. Yet it was agreed that an inferior beast usually cost almost as much to keep as a good one. Bakewell began in the obvious way, by breeding only from what looked like the best animals – in a flock of sheep from the best ewes and rams. Secondly, he decided beforehand whether 'best' meant best for mutton or best for wool. Other breeders of his day had got as far as that. But Bakewell then went on to do another thing, which is what modern breeders do. He waited to see what sort of lambs, and also how many, his 'best-looking' rams and ewes produced: this is known as 'progeny selection'. When he had got a ram which not only looked good but whose sons and daughters turned out well, he would refuse to sell him, though he was often offered huge prices for such a ram.

At breeding sheep for mutton, no one could beat Bakewell. A breed descended from his 'Border Leicesters' are still famous. They are handsome, if curious-looking beasts, as the picture shows, and the rams still fetch top prices wherever fat lambs are raised. If the reader had a nice roast of New Zealand lamb last Sunday, that lamb was very likely a 'cross', and had somewhere in its pedigree a descendant of a ram from Robert Bakewell's Border Leicester flock. Most of the distinctive and highly specialized breeds of farm animals today have been bred by Bakewell's method of 'progeny selection'.

Finally the Norfolk tenant farmers admitted that Townshend, Bakewell, Tull, Young and Coke were right. There had been an old saying: 'Throw your hat on to a ripening barley crop; if the hat rests on the top, the crop is good'. The local farmers, who were at last enthusiastic, told Coke, ''Tis all hat-barley since the horse-drill came'.

Every year at the time of sheep-shearing, Coke and his wife gave a feast in their splendid house, Holkham. The cheerfulness and jollifications attracted visitors and did a lot to reconcile the opposers of the new farming methods. There were prizes such as silver bowls and tankards for the best sheep, or for something new in the way of a harrow or horse-drill. Two farmers out of Kent and Sussex told how Squire Coke showed his crops, let them measure his bulls, showed his dairy and his sheep:

'three thousand acres without a fence farmed in a very capital style; yearling heifers fed on a very rich salt-marsh, and rams so uncommonly fat it would be vain for them to waddle away from us.'

Mrs Coke would often ride thirty miles to show visitors round if her husband was busy.

Border Leicesters are popular in New Zealand. Bakewell, who popularized these odd, Roman-nosed sheep, was the shrewdest breeder of all. More in the text.

This ram is a Merino. The breed made fortunes in Australia. New breeds of sheep were bred for mutton or wool, to suit lush land or sparse hill pasture.

The milk of such Jersey cows is much richer than that of other breeds.

What is the true wealth of nations?
1750–1800

Both in Chelsea and Dresden such pretty, slightly silly, shepherds and shepherdesses were produced. The blossoms were usually cast in clay, one by one, or even petal by petal, and then put into place.

This richly panelled room (from Norfolk House, now at the Victoria and Albert Museum) was called 'The Music Room' because of the gilded bas-reliefs of musical instruments used in the decoration.

These changes amounted to an 'agricultural revolution', and though they made for national prosperity they also meant hardship for some people because of the enclosure of what had been common land. Cottagers who had had the right to pasture a cow or a goat on the common were given little or no compensation:

'The law arrests the man or woman
Who steals the goose from off the common,
But leaves the greater villain loose
Who steals the common from the goose.'

Many poor country people no longer had a place on the land. Arthur Young, then celebrated as a writer on the new farming, believed there was real despair and that some sort of 'welfare' or public help was called for. He comments:

'If you talk to them about their improvidence, they will ask, "For whom am I to save? If I am sober, shall I have land for a cow? You offer no motive".'

The fact is that this land improvement was going on blindly. The study of economics, then often called 'political arithmetic', had hardly begun. Adam Smith's famous *The Wealth of Nations* was almost the first book on the subject and was published late in the 1770s. (Adam Smith was one of the Scotsmen who helped to give the Glasgow and Edinburgh of the time their brilliant reputation.)

Adam Smith argued that competition between individual producers, and their efforts to make improvements, enriched the community and were the true 'wealth of nations'. The Government's job was not to make regulations about 'just prices and fair wages'. This was an out-of-date idea and interference was harmful. Adam Smith would, however, never have gone as far as his followers, who later gleefully declared that, even if people were starving, it would be wrong to interfere with the 'play of the market' and the 'laws of supply and demand' by feeding them. Many employers such as Whitbread the brewer, Wedgwood the potter, and Robert Owen the cotton manufacturer, never agreed with this 'utilitarianism', but for long most businessmen did. So there was no 'Welfare' and most of the great

'Infirm of purpose! Give me the daggers,' cried Mrs Siddons.

1750–1780

wealth-bringing changes of the next aventurious years were made as roughly as the surgical operations of the day.

As for the fashionable life of the time, it was an odd mixture. Elegant young men often wore pink-and-white make-up, and carried large fur muffs, while the ladies simpered, piled up their own and borrowed hair, and then had the whole powdered and ornamented prodigiously with feathers, ribbons and jewels. Manners swung between extreme politeness – all bows and curtseys – and a roughness and rudeness that would disgrace a pub-brawl of today. Here is an example from the novel *Evelina*, whose author, Fanny Burney (her picture is on this page) was an observant, sensible, rather shy young lady of what was called 'good family'.

Evelina, her aunt, her uncle 'the Captain' and an elderly French lady are all coming back in a coach from Ranelagh Pleasure Gardens. The French lady has missed her escort:

'Pray,' said the Captain, 'why did you go to a public place without an Englishman?' Madame Duval exclaimed tearfully, 'I'll go back to France as fast as I can.' 'Ay, do', cried he, 'and then go to the devil together, for that's the fittest voyage for the French.' Soon Madame Duval called him a 'low, dirty fellow'. 'Dirty fellow!' (exclaimed the Captain, seizing both her wrists) 'Hark you, Mrs Frog, you'd best hold your tongue! If you don't I shall make no ceremony of tripping you out of the window, and there you may lie in the mud till some of your Monseers come to help you out of it.'

Theatres were popular. But King George III was a simple soul and didn't like Shakespeare's plays at all. He complained bitterly one day to his wife's lady-in-waiting, this same Fanny Burney:

'Was there ever such stuff as a great part of Shakespeare? Only one must not say so! What? Is there not sad stuff? What? What? – Oh, I know it is not to be said! But it's true! Only it's Shakespeare, and nobody dare abuse him.'

Smart audiences, however, flocked to see Shakespeare's plays, especially when some famous actor or actress played the lead. David Garrick was one of the stars. Mrs Siddons was another. When she played Lady Macbeth the whole theatre grew still with awe. When she was famous she wrote about the night on which she first learned the part:

'I shut myself up as usual, when all the family were retired, and commenced my study. As the character is very short, I thought I should soon accomplish it. I went on with tolerable composure, in the silence of the night (a night I never can forget), till I came to the murder-scene when the horror of it rose to a degree that made it impossible for me to get farther. I snatched up my candle, and hurried out of the room in a paroxysm of terror. My dress was of silk, and the rustling of it, as I went up the stairs to go to bed, seemed to my panic-struck fancy like the movement of a spectre pursuing me.'

Though London was important and though travelling was so slow and rough and though Dr Johnson could make his famous remark: 'Sir, whoever is tired of London is tired of life', London was only the centre of a great trade network, a city from which fleets set out. Other ports and towns were vital in British life.

We have already told the tale of two unsuccessful efforts to meet the challenge of a dreadful in-shore danger, the

Miss Fanny Burney, novelist and lady-in-waiting. Such hats and even larger ones were fashionable.

David Garrick was both an immensely popular actor, and a theatre manager.

Mrs. Siddons became the most famous tragic actress of her day.

Prefabrication and the ingenious Mr Smeaton
1750–1780

At last an Eddystone Lighthouse that would stand up to all the dangers. Smeaton had each stone shaped and numbered. In fact this was a prefabricated job.

Eddystone reef, off one of them. Now at last came methods that marked new ways. John Smeaton, the man with the modern outlook, was born near Leeds in 1724 and Samuel Smiles, in his book *Lives of the Engineers,* describes how when Smeaton was a boy, the raw wool and finished cloth travelled to and from Leeds in a very old-fashioned way – on the backs of pack-horses, or, quite often, women.

Smeaton studied civil engineering, and when the Admiralty's special lighthouse body, 'the Brethren of Trinity House', consulted the Royal Society on what to do next about this troublesome Eddystone (see page 100) the Royal Society advised them to call in Smeaton.

The young Yorkshireman took coach to Plymouth, had a sailing boat put at his disposal, stayed in Plymouth a fortnight and, in that time, managed only fifteen hours on the reef, two hours of low tide on fine days. He stayed on longer, but it was another two weeks before he could so much as get on it again.

When Smeaton got back to London he made, with his own hands, a complete scale model of a lighthouse for the Trinity House Committee. He told them that he wanted to build in stone. This was a new idea; in fact all his ideas were new, and he had a hard job to get the Committee to agree. He set out for Plymouth again, stopping on the way to arrange for supplies of granite and Portland stone to be sent to Plymouth. Next he hired a

work-yard in which the stone could be dressed and shaped; then he arranged for vessels to carry men, tools and later, the great, heavy, dressed stones out to the reef. All this nearly amounted to what is still new today – 'prefabrication'. On the afternoon of 3rd August, 1756, he and his masons managed to land at low tide.

'From that time forward the work proceeded, though with many interruptions caused by bad weather and heavy seas. When the weather was favourable, the men worked by torchlight. The principal object of the first season was to get the dovetail recesses cut out of the rock for the reception of the foundation-stones.'

Smeaton had planned everything beforehand. For instance, he arranged for the *Neptune* (a two-masted barge-like craft) to be anchored as near the rock as was safe, to act as a store-vessel and living-quarters. So, when weather and tide allowed, his masons could get to work at once for their two hours of low tide. For days it often happened that the men could not work at all; the reader can imagine how difficult it was to get heavy blocks of stone off a rolling, plunging boat and on to the reef. Meantime in the work-yard, a second gang had been getting on with cutting the stone blocks and numbering each one. Because of the danger of losing a block overboard, as they tried to get it on to the rock, Smeaton arranged that a wooden model of each stone should be kept in the work-yard, so that an exact replacement could be made at once.

There were again man-made hindrances. Smeaton's masons were sometimes seized by the Press Gang when they came ashore, so Trinity House had a badge made for each one, giving them exemption.

After all, and in spite of all, almost incredibly, John Smeaton and his men triumphed and, in October 1759, the new light shone out for the first time. It is difficult to know which to admire most, Smeaton's entirely modern way of organizing, or his and his men's courage. It can be imagined how utterly wet and miserable life on board the pitching *Neptune* must have been as she rode at her anchors through those storms. Smeaton shared all the anxiety and danger.

There is plenty of courage and daring in the tales of those years.

Of the famous explorers of the time, one at least can be really admired, though the famous Dampier, whose account of his voyages became a best-seller, and Anson were in many ways ruffians. Dampier had been a pirate for eleven of the years of his famous explorations, while Anson, who sailed round the world between 1740 and 1744, was only a little better. They were brave, good navigators and kept records that were a great help to later captains, but they were ferocious to their enemies and often cruel to their crews. Captain Cook was a different kind of man. He was as good, or better, professionally than Dampier or Anson, and a decent, upright human being by any standard. In New Zealand and Australia, Cook is rightly held as a great hero, so much so, that, in the schools there, they get almost tired of hearing of his courage, skill and humanity.

James Cook was born in Yorkshire near Whitby. He was first apprenticed to a grocer, but later went to sea at 15, and helped chart the St. Lawrence River for Wolfe's famous surprise capture of Quebec. He was soon promoted to the command of the brig *Endeavour*, his duty being to chart, and, because the Royal Society had a hand in the arrangements, on his first voyage he had with him a team of naturalists under Sir Joseph Banks, of whom the most notable was a pupil of the

famous Swedish botanist Linnaeus, a fat, short, cheerful Swede named Solander.

Captain Cook is often thought of as the discoverer of Australia and New Zealand. In fact both had been touched on before, notably by the Dutch explorer Tasman, and occasionally by whaling crews going ashore for water and timber. But it was Cook who charted the coasts. The passage between the two islands of New Zealand is called Cook Straits, for sailing back and forth from there he made charts of nearly 3,000 miles of coast.

While he was busy at this his naturalist passengers were ashore collecting plants and insects. This first voyage ended well. Cook, following up the work of a naval surgeon, James Lind, made the discovery that scurvy, a disease that took a frightful toll at sea, could be prevented by providing crews with fresh food. (It is now known that scurvy is caused by a shortage of the trace-element, Vitamin 'C'.) Cook's crews were in all ways treated better than most seamen of the time; that is, they were worked less hard, and were given a chance to get dry after inevitable drenchings. A second of Cook's voyages also ended well. In both these, and on a third, in which, alas, Cook was killed, he had the advantage of using the new, really good timepiece, Harrison's Chronometer (see illustration on page 115).

Captain Cook and Smeaton are examples of the sort of men who were beginning to make a mark. Josiah Wedgwood a potter,

Icebergs, kiwis, kangaroos, and coral reefs! Was there a great unknown continent south of the equator? That great navigator Captain Cook found Australia to be a great island, and New Zealand two smaller mountainous islands. This and much else he proved. Cook's *Endeavour* took no harm among these formidable icebergs, but was dangerously holed on a sharp coral pinnacle off the coast of Australia.

The scientists who sailed with Cook found living things that were strange to them amongst the corals of the Great Barrier Reef.

Shall there be no taxation without representation?

1750–1780

This fine public building is in Williamsburg, Virginia. The town has been carefully restored and is rightly now much visited by Americans interested in their own country. The picture makes it clear that Virginians were (by about 1704) men of taste and by no means poor.

This was what happened on the evening of what was soon called 'The Boston Tea Party'! The young men of Boston were as angry as the members of the Assembly at Williamsburg at being told to pay taxes about which they hadn't been consulted. When this East-Indiaman had docked, a crowd of young men, painted and disguised as Indian Braves, pitched the taxed tea-chests into the harbour.

Samuel Whitbread a brewer, Joseph Priestley a scientist and Nonconformist minister, Benjamin Franklin a printer from New England, Abraham Darby a Quaker iron-founder, and Robert Owen a mill-manager, were others.

Some of these 'new men' took hardly any notice of politics (Humphry Davy the famous chemist, Captain Cook, Michael Faraday, the first to induce an electric current with a magnet, and John Dalton, who weighed elements, for instance). Some were passionately interested in reform. But they all had this in common, they set about their various jobs in an orderly way, charting, experimenting, making models, planning ahead.

Many of them, however, held 're-forming' opinions because of personal experiences or professional knowledge. As a decent and experienced employer, for instance, Wedgwood believed that the slave-trade was wicked.

Priestley was very much a reformer. This great chemist (the composition of 'common air' and other gases were his chief interest) took an active part in politics because his work had suffered on account of his being a Nonconformist minister. Priestley believed that liberty for men, both black and white, was important.

As for Benjamin Franklin he was not only the discoverer (by way of a simple, dangerous experiment) of the fact that lightning is electrical, and thunder the immense, echoing crackle of a huge electrical discharge, but – because he *was* an American and, since the colonies were now demanding more freedom – like Priestley, he took a vivid interest in liberty and human rights. Of the pictures on this page, that of Williamsburg is here to suggest how civilized some of the American colonies had become. That of the 'Boston Tea Party' foretells the trouble that was soon to come – a quarrel which was to lead to war, a war which all Benjamin Franklin's efforts, his eloquence, jokes, and world-wide scientific reputation, were not enough to prevent.

This was the time of canal-digging in England, because most of the roads were so very bad that canals were, for a whole

Dukes, canals, pottery and machinery

Without canals and with the roads so hopelessly churned up, it would have been impossible to move heavy goods like coal and iron-ore. On the Barton aqueduct a canal and its towpath cross a river.

generation and more, 'the arteries of the Industrial Revolution'.

Josiah Wedgwood, the master potter, employed the very best designers for his elegant pottery. He also realized that, if he was going to sell his heavy, breakable wares out of Burslem and Stoke-on-Trent at reasonable prices, there must be more up-to-date transport than pack-horses. The Duke of Bridgewater, who had coal mines on his estates, found it shockingly inefficient and expensive for his coal to have to travel by wagon or pack-horse on roads deep in mud all winter. Water transport would be a huge saving. Both the Duke and the potter therefore promoted canals, while an ingenious Scotsman named Brindley laid out the levels and became one of the most famous of the canal engineers.

The picture shows better than words what a difficult job it was when laying out a canal to get the levels right. There had of course to be locks and tunnels through hills, as well as underpasses and high aqueducts such as these at the Barton crossing. In a fascinating book *British Canals*, Mr Charles Hadfield explains that towns all over the world have usually grown up on river banks. A river had its

mills, every quarter mile or so, for milling corn, fulling cloth, driving the hammers of ironworks. This hindered barges for each mill regulated the flow of water by means of a mill pond and weir.

Going upstream on a river, the waters of which were held back as each miller needed it, a heavy barge would often go aground. Then the bargee would have to walk to the mill above, and bargain with the owner for a 'flash' – enough water to be released to raise the river level and so free the barge. Barge-masters might have to send ten or twenty miles ahead and pay extra fees and tips for a 'flash'. Fast-flowing rivers, notably the Severn with its tidal-bore, had other hazards.

No wonder that the tremendous work of digging canals was worth while. When the canals were at their most developed they carried passengers as well as coal, pottery and salt. Time-tables were issued and there were cabin boats in which the passengers were given newspapers and refreshments. A contemporary picture shows the horses on the tow-path drawing a 'swift' boat at the gallop. Those who did the pick and shovel work when the canals were being dug, were nicknamed 'navvies' – from 'Inland Navigation'.

Mrs. Josiah Wedgwood. Notice her beautifully piled hair. Below, Dr Priestley, the famous chemist.

111

How honourable was The Honourable East India Company?
1750–1795

A caricature of an Indian and a European playing chess. Badly as the English behaved in India, there was at least less nonsense about a colour-bar.

Indian factions were often backed by rival Europeans. This venerable gentleman's soldiers are dressed in European-style tunics.

While all this was going on the Honourable East India Company was fast establishing a regular kingdom in Northern India. India had seemed a fabulous country of idol-filled temples and great marble palaces with courts that bubbled with fountains, of ruby-mines, of princes in cloth of gold sewn with pearls, who rode on jewelled elephants.

Waves of invaders from Persia or Afghanistan had swept down upon it; but for the last two hundred years the invasions had almost stopped. Northern India (roughly what is now the Punjab, Bengal and East Pakistan) had been ruled from Delhi by the Mogul Emperors. These Moguls were Muslims but the inhabitants of the country were mostly Hindus. Now, in the middle of the 1700s, there were troubles between rulers and ruled and more attacks from outside; the great Mogul Empire was breaking up. British, French, Portuguese and Dutch merchants had for long had trading-posts along the coasts. Each 'East India Company' also had a private army. All four, especially the French and British, now began to back first one native faction and then another. The British had, in their brilliant Robert Clive, a particularly able and unscrupulous general who made no bones about using force, about enriching himself and letting his officers do the same. Adam Smith (see page 106) said that Clive's rule was 'perhaps the worst of all governments for any country whatsoever'. Horace Walpole, the Prime Minister's fashionable son, agreed:

'We have outdone the Spaniards in Peru. They were at least butchers on a religious principle. We have murdered, deposed, plundered, usurped!'

British sea-power enabled us to beat all comers at this sort of robbery.

Fortunately there were many people in England who disapproved and who cared for the peoples of India. Unfortunately the rights and wrongs of the 'India question' became squabbling-points for Whigs and Tories. The Government did, however, at last intervene in the affairs of the East India Company, but the first Governor-General of India, Warren Hastings, who had done

Ruffians, pleasing and unpleasing, in high places and low.

his best, was dragged through a trial for misgovernment that lasted seven years.

Both Whigs and Tories behaved badly in India. But home standards of honesty in Britain were also shocking. Ministers of State took bribes, yet for ordinary stealing punishments were savage. In defiance of all our boasted liberties the Admiralty continually sent out their press-gangs. His Majesty's ships were horrible with disease, especially scurvy, the food was bad and scanty, and the officers and petty officers ill-treated and flogged their wretched half-starved men into 'doing their duty', a duty which they had never agreed to do. Country squires gambled and drank, the Westminster magistrates made what they could out of fines, and we can scarcely think of a three-cornered hat without being reminded of highwaymen, smugglers and pirates.

Far the most unpleasant of all the ruffians were the Wreckers. All round the coast there were villages whose inhabitants' favourite way of making a living was wrecking. False lights were shown ashore to lure vessels to their destruction: once a ship was on the rocks, any unfortunate sailor who tried to get ashore would be deliberately battered to death. Dead men tell no tales.

There was never an amusing 'musical' about these brutes, but Gay's *Beggar's Opera*, a cheerful satire on statesmen and lesser ruffians, had for some time been one of the theatre's great successes. The scenes are disreputable inns, gaming-houses, or prisons. The music is charming. The hero, a highwayman, has carelessly married two of his numerous girls, and there is not one respectable character in the whole romp. Indeed when there is a question of what happened to various 'Personages of the Drama' the audience is told that 'they were all either transported or hanged'. An old informer and receiver of stolen goods sings:

'Through all the Employments of life
All Professions be-rogue one another:
The Priest calls the Lawyer a Cheat,
The Lawyer be-knaves the Divine:
And the Statesman, because he's so great,
Thinks his Trade is as honest as mine!'

Edward Teach, alias 'Black Beard' the notorious pirate, was famous for twisting 'slow matches' into his hair and then setting them alight.

She has been lured on to the rocks by false lights. As dawn breaks the wreckers are gutting her.

'Your money or your life!'

Does dabbling in the dew make milkmaids pretty?
1717–1800

Newcomen's steam-pumping engine. They called it 'The Engine for Raising Water with a Power made by Fire'.

Michael Faraday, who discovered the principle of the dynamo.

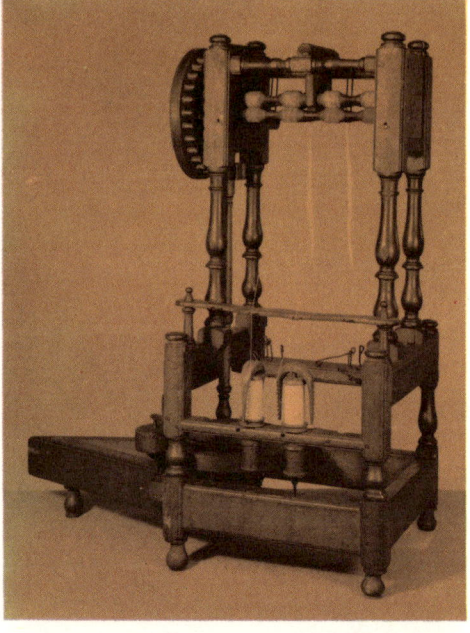

Arkwright's and Kay's spinning machine. This worked by water power, and spun a cotton thread strong enough for both warp and weft, so that linen was no longer needed for the warp.

The reader may think it a relief to turn from ruffians and savage laws to constructive characters such as scientists, and to some of the reformers who were trying to make England into something more like a Christian country. One picture on this page is of Michael Faraday, the charming bookbinder's apprentice who changed over to being lab-boy to Sir Humphry Davy, the celebrated chemist, because he believed that scientists told the truth and were not to be bribed. Another was the equally charming Edward Jenner. At first a pupil of William Hunter the great surgeon in London, Jenner went home to Gloucestershire to be a country doctor, and, working on four facts, made a great advance in the prevention of infectious disease. Fact one: Milkmaids were pretty. Why? 'Dabbling in the dew makes milkmaids fair'? Jenner wondered if it wasn't because their faces were not pitted with smallpox. Milkmaids didn't catch smallpox, this was fact two. . . . What they did catch was an infectious breaking-out on their hands called 'cowpox', this was fact three. Fact four was that the dangerous smallpox 'inoculation' worked fairly well. Suppose, thought Jenner, 'vaccination', that is to say inoculation with cow-pox, would do instead? It worked, and it works to this day.

Many of the excellent people of this time became reformers because they believed that pickpockets, wreckers, highwaymen, receivers, as well as the bribetakers and enforcers of savage laws, had become bad for lack of Christian teaching. The mighty preachers, Wesley and Whitefield, used to travel, month after month, round the country and to thrill huge congregations at open-air revival meetings and bring about countless conversions.

Mrs Elizabeth Fry, the Quaker, when she was still quite young, found that she had what Quakers call 'a concern' about the wretched state of women prisoners and their children. She went first to see Newgate: 'Three hundred women with their children were huddled together in two wards and two cells . . . they had no night clothes or bedclothes' and no facilities for cooking, washing or eating. But

Could he prove that he owned the 'poor African'?

they could drink. The governor was afraid to go in. Not so Elizabeth Fry.

John Howard, a dissenter, gave his whole life to trying to get some sort of prison reform both here and abroad. Samuel Romilly brought bill after bill before Parliament in his efforts to make the laws less savage. There were no less than two hundred 'crimes' for which men women, and even children could be, and were, hanged, while the horrible punishment of 'hanging, drawing and quartering' was still legal.

None of these people saw much result from all their work and hopes. Yet now, in all civilized countries, there have been just the sort of reforms for which they pleaded. However, there is a great deal still to be done, and a body called 'the Howard League' tries (often in vain) to see that it is done in Britain.

The slave trade had long been active and, like the prisons and the hangings, it had begun to shock decent opinion. It often came very close home to quite ordinary home-keeping people. This story is told by Samuel Smiles (see also page 108). There limped into young Dr. Sharp's back-street free surgery, near the London Docks, a miserable, starved-looking black man. He had been brought as a slave from Barbados and so brutally treated by his master (a lawyer) that, though still young, he seemed like an old man. Now lame, almost blind, and unable to work, his master had turned him out into the streets to starve. The doctor and his brother, Granville Sharp, a young clerk, had pity, treated his injuries, fed him and, when he was better, got him a place as odd-job man with the wife of a chemist. On an unlucky day Jonathan, 'the poor African', went out with her to the market, the Barbados lawyer passed by, recognized him, saw that he was fit for work again, claimed him as 'strayed property' and cunningly sold him for a good sum to a man who was just off back to Barbados again. Jonathan, in terrible distress, somehow managed to get word to Granville Sharp. Jonathan's new owner kept repeating, during one law case after another, that 'the nigger' was his private property, and that he had the receipt for the money.

Right and wrong were clear; not so the law; negro slaves were still openly sold in many English cities, Bristol, Liverpool, and London among them, and rewards were offered for the recapture of runaway slaves. Granville Sharp had no money for lawyers to fight for poor Jonathan against cunning barristers or against kidnappers in the London docks who ran a trade in catching such 'niggers'. However, there was some decency even in that murky world. This case ended well and Jonathan was finally rescued by these excellent brothers. Thereafter Granville Sharp saved many more slaves in London, and at last, Lord Mansfield, the Lord Chief Justice, declared, in the case of another African called Somerset, that on the soil of Britain no man could legally be a slave to another.

Overseas, other battles for freedom were being fought, and, as in the case of slavery, some people in England took one side, some another. This time the question was, had each of the 'Assemblies' of the American colonists the same rights as the British Houses of Parliament? Spain, France and Portugal had never allowed their colonists any self-government: they were firmly ruled from home. But English colonists took for granted that they had a right to be consulted when decisions were made. There were, by now, thirteen English colonies strung along the American coast, each self-governing. Further north, in what is now Canada, were French colonies. If the English colonists wanted to spread, the natural thing was for them to spread west inland, but how could they if the French, with whom the British were nearly always at war, were colonizing all down the great river Mississippi which flows into the Gulf of Mexico? Many towns and cities there have French names to this day – New Orleans (of jazz fame,) Baton Rouge and so on. The English colonists didn't like this southern move of the French, and armies were sent from Britain to defend them. Wolfe's famous capture of Quebec was part of this war, a war which, though successful, cost a lot of money.

'Am I not a man and a brother?' Wedgwood distributed replicas of this famous little plaque free.

These irons were made red-hot and the unfortunate slaves, men, women and children, were branded with their new owner's initials.

Harrison's first chronometer was large and clumsy. Finally, he made one not much bigger than a pocket watch. It kept perfect time so at last navigating officers could tell their latitude by timing the sun.

A scientist turned statesman pleads for common sense
1760–1789

Totem-pole carved by Indians of what is now British Columbia. The faces represent the spirits of the tribe.

It seemed fair to King George III and his advisers that the colonists should help to pay for the armies which had defended them. They clapped taxes on many kinds of goods entering the American colonies, but did not ask the colonists their opinion. 'No taxation without representation,' the colonists protested. Today, historians think that what made the colonies refuse was this one fact: they were not asked, but *required*, to pay.

George III and the stupid Lord North, his Prime Minister, in fact treated the American 'assemblies' much as Charles I and Strafford (see page 71) had treated the British Parliament and with similar results.

The Whigs who had ruled Britain for so long, were at this time out of office, so the King and Lord North (right-wing Tories) refused to consult officially with the colonists' own assemblies. An interesting man, who has already been spoken of as a scientist, now took a hand and came to England as an envoy, to try to reason with the government. This was Benjamin Franklin (see page 110). He preached a Puritan morality in his book, *Poor Richard's Almanach*, but he was also a really eminent and original scientist and a famous joker. He pleaded in England most eloquently for a sensible settlement; at the same time he amused himself – and all the Whig statesmen and reformers who thoroughly sympathized with the colonists – by proving how little the English knew about America; for instance by telling people in London, with a perfectly straight face, that one of the most splendid sights in America was to see the whales jumping up Niagara Falls, as they chased the cod-fish. He was actually believed.

War with the American colonies came. The king and his advisers could hardly have behaved more stupidly. Washington and Jefferson, two great American leaders, helped by an army from France led by the Marquis de La Fayette, beat them. The American Republic was born.

There were a great many Englishmen to welcome the new nation. In fact, most of those whose names come in here as 'constructors' or 'reformers' did so.

Priestley, William Blake, Whitbread, to give only a few instances, as well as a great many other people who believed in the current Whig principles – the Whigs being at that time much less stiff in their ideas than the Tories – very much disliked the way George III and 'the King's Friends' (his little clique in Parliament) were running the country. A deservedly popular historian of today, Roger Fulford, points out how general in England was this feeling that the American fight was for liberty against tyranny, with King George III on the wrong side.
'This idea is shown over and over again in the pages of Horace Walpole [the man of fashion].

'When the rift between the two English-speaking peoples was completed, he wrote, "If England is free, and America is free, though disunited, the whole earth will not be in vassalage".'

Now the reader may have noticed that it was just said that the Americans had been helped to independence by a general with a French name leading a French Army and may well think this sentence odd. Why should a French army have been helping in a revolt against a King? Why were they helping to found a brand-new republic whose leaders had solemnly declared that 'all men are born equal', and who demanded that everyone should have a right to 'life, liberty and the pursuit of happiness'?

The French had, for long, had an absolute monarchy, and the whole social set-up rested on the idea that men were certainly not born equal: on the contrary they were born to be nobles or peasants, for instance, and some French peasants were still serfs. The motive of the French in helping the Americans was rivalry with and hatred of Britain. The important point is that this helping of the American colonies to found their republic cost the French government much money. French taxes were already so high and the way of collecting them so inefficient, that now King Louis XVI could hardly raise enough to carry on the government. Some historians today believe that this extraordinary American adventure was the last straw that finally bankrupted the French government. One finance minister

After the storming of the Bastille, Europe was changed.

after another was called in by poor anxious King Louis XVI. They raised loans, they tried all sorts of dodges, but at last even the celebrated Swiss banker, Necker, told Louis that, in the emergency, he would have to call the Estates General (more or less comparable to our Parliament) and see if they would vote him more taxes.

Since this is a history of 'Life in England' it would be out of place to tell in any detail the thrilling and often alarming story of the French Revolution and of the rise of Napoleon Bonaparte. But what must be told is how every up and down in the struggle, and each argument used by those who were struggling, echoed and reverberated in England for the next fifty years, much as it did in the rest of Europe. It would not be much of an exaggeration to say that, after 1789 when the Bastille was stormed (the old sullen fortress in which Voltaire had once been imprisoned), and when its doors had been flung open, Europe was never the same again.

'How much the greatest event in the history of the world and how much the best,' said Charles James Fox, the Whig statesman, when the first news of the Revolution came. But in a couple of years, after the trial and execution of the French King and Queen, respectable opinion in England changed. Refugee aristocrats came over to England with terrible tales. The Tories panicked. Where was this sort of thing going to end? Britain declared war on Revolutionary France. But the poet Blake, the great Priestley and Tom Paine, who wrote *The Rights of Man*, thought that the former French government had been tyrannical, that the French King's party had been a danger and that his execution had been as just as that of Charles I.

Priestley had his laboratory smashed up, his scientific papers destroyed and had to fly to America. The fact is that the respectable people of England had bad consciences and gradually became more and more frightened. They had not listened to Romilly, Howard or Elizabeth Fry (see page 115), or to the sailors at Spithead or the Nore, who had mutinied

The Royal Institution. Here Humphry Davy and later Faraday had their laboratories. The building has a fine library and lecture-theatre which these two made famous. It was founded by Sir Joseph Banks and an eccentric but very practical inventor, Count Rumford, who amongst other things advocated pressure-cookers and double glazing.

Brutal floggings were common on naval ships. Food was bad, the men's pay behindhand, and at last, at Spithead and on the Nore, the sailors mutinied. This was while Nelson was still only a young officer.

Express mail-coaches bring exciting news
1789–1805

'Going down with Victory'. This time the news was not of Peninsular battles, but of peace after Waterloo.

Water for the coach horses.

and refused to take the Fleet to sea, and on whose courage England had so long depended. The men of the lower deck were still scandalously treated; the picture and caption on page 117 suggest what was going on.

All over Europe this alarm at such sudden demands by 'the lower orders' was even greater, for there was far less liberty. Six governments went to war with Revolutionary France, and France gathered armies of defence. One who organized such a 'popular' army was a small, pale, young artillery officer from Corsica, and *The Marseillaise* was one of the tunes to which another of the armies marched.

Yet it is possible to know a great deal about ordinary life in many parts of Britain without realizing anything about that first enthusiasm for the Revolution, the change of feeling, or even about the war. This may have been because news took days or weeks to reach distant counties, or because so much that was interesting was going on here, including some real improvements.

Take a minor instance; there has already been a good deal in this history about roads whose mud would suck the shoes off the horses' hoofs. By the early 1800s a few main roads had been improved and kept up by commercial companies – 'Turnpike Trusts' – which charged tolls. Bowling along on one of these new main roads, on the box-seat of one of the new mail coaches, was a thrilling experience. In London, at 8 o' clock in the morning, the mail-coaches started from the head Post Office in Lombard Street. De Quincey, (a writer famous for his gorgeous style) tells how the names of the cities for which they were bound were called:

'Great ancestral names, known to history through a thousand years – Lincoln, Winchester, Portsmouth, Gloucester, Oxford, Bristol, Manchester, York, Newcastle, Edinburgh, Glasgow, Perth, Stirling, Aberdeen! Our coaches filled the street, though a long one, and though we were drawn up in double file. On any night the spectacle was beautiful from the absolute perfection of all the appointments about the carriages and the harness,

'Fire racing along a train of gun powder'

their brilliant cleanliness, the magnificence of the horses. Every part of every carriage – wheels, axles, linch-pins, pole, glasses, lamps – had been cleaned, every horse had been groomed.'

Britain was as usual at war with France at the time de Quincey is describing, a war that was being fought at sea and also in Spain and Portugal. These mail-coaches brought the newpapers with the latest war-news and when there had been a victory the coaches were decked out, so the first sight of a decked-out coach gave the first news.

'Behold! To the ordinary display, what a heartshaking addition! Horses, men, carriages, all are dressed in laurels and flowers, oak-leaves and ribbons! All night long and all next day many of these Mails will be like fire racing along a train of gunpowder.'

It wasn't the same French Revolutionary government that Britain was fighting now. Because France had had a hard time in defending herself, it was now a soldier who was in command. What a soldier! Europe shook! At first it was just a young, pale lieutenant of the Revolutionary army – Napoleon Bonaparte. Very soon it was 'Colonel', then 'General', then 'Consul' Bonaparte, and then, last, 'His Majesty the Emperor Napoleon'. When that happened it was the turn of a good many former sympathizers with the French Revolution to turn away in anger and disappointment. Beethoven, the great composer, for instance, tore up the dedication of the Concerto he had written in Bonaparte's honour, because he now believed that Bonaparte had traded his faith for a crown. But some people in Europe, (that great novelist Stendhal, for instance) believed that this Napoleon, though he was both a great cynic and a restless soldier, this Emperor, this earth-shaking conqueror, was doing more good than harm. Very few people in England thought so. For one thing he was massing a big and well-trained army, complete with invasion-barges, at Boulogne. Even apart from that, this difference in feeling would really have been quite natural. On the Continent, where there was still serfdom and imprisonment at the whim

Turner's magnificent picture of French and English men-of-war fighting off Cape Trafalgar.

Admiral Nelson. A life-sized wax figure modelled by Catherine Andras. It is dressed in the clothes he had worn, and the likeness was said to be perfect.

How many could read the news when Napoleon struck again?
1780–1812

A comparatively well-equipped comfortable school in which a few girls were also taught. The children's slates hang under the tables and texts for reading on the walls. An open fire warms the school room.

The Bench of Judges by Hogarth. 'A terrible show', Gay's highwayman, Captain MacHeath, had said earlier, of those who judged him.

of some fat princeling in a powdered wig, Napoleon really had brought in codes of decent laws. So in spite of all the horrible sufferings of war, he could be seen as a liberator.

Again and again Napoleon kept beating the allied governments of Europe in battles on land and the only vital thing that prevented his invasion of England was the British Navy. So, for us, the most vital news carried by the coaches was the news from the fleet. One October morning in 1805 they were once more splendidly decked, but they showed, as well as scarlet, gold and laurel, funeral wreaths and black mourning streamers. They carried the news of what became the most famous sea-victory in Britain's history, the great sea-fight off Cape Trafalgar. The black streamers were for Lord Nelson, the Navy's best-loved and greatest Admiral, who had been killed in the moment of victory. This victory, Trafalgar, meant that for Napoleon to try to lead his army into England would be madly imprudent, yet it by no means meant that he was finally defeated. Now he struck out again, with his unbeaten armies, right and left at the old Continental kingdoms. He believed he could strangle England, for he now had the power to prevent any of the old kingdoms from trading with her. Now and then, during these Napoleonic wars, there were peace treaties, notably one signed at Amiens in 1802. But no such peace lasted long; a year, two years at the most.

De Quincey tells his readers that the mail coaches brought newspapers, which brings up the question of who could read and who couldn't. The answer is that about half the boys and young men could, but perhaps only a quarter of the women and girls. This may sound a poor percentage, but it did mean that about three and a half million children had somehow been taught their letters. How had this been done? Not systematically for sure, except in Scotland where there was already a state school system. In England there were Dame schools, and also orphanages, where the boys and girls were taught to read, write and sing. But neither Dame schools nor orphanages

'Brutish, gross ignorance about salvation'

covered the whole population.

Here and there other kinds of schools grew up.

'In divers places throughout England (where there were no charity-schools) several poor children are taught to read at the expense of the minister and some of the richer inhabitants of the parish, reported a follower of the Reverend Griffith Jones, who tackled schooling in an ingenious way. To begin with he used some of his church collections for hiring teachers. Such money would have gone nowhere if he had spent it on building a school. He used it only to pay teachers. One of these would go to a district, find some leading and sympathetic inhabitant who would lend a room, and there a school would be run for two or three months in the summer for both grown-up people and children. After a while the teacher would move on and start another school. These 'circulating schools' became famous. It was shrewd psychology, for we all probably react to a 'now is your chance', and the fact that the school-master was going to move on, made people crowd into the bare little rooms. Soon a powerful religious and educational body, The Society for Promoting Christian Knowledge, began to help. (The 'circulating schools' had all along bought their books from them). The 'circulating' and all the other 'schools for the poor' taught the catechism and were very much influenced by various religious beliefs.

Education was further mixed up with religion because neither dissenters nor Catholics could go to universities. So both trained their own ministers or priests at 'Dissenting Academies, or seminaries. What was taught at Oxford and Cambridge and the public schools – Eton, Harrow, Winchester, Charterhouse, for example – had got into a rut; the schools were by now old-fashioned or downright scandalous. The boys often ran wild, drinking, swearing, and 'barring out' the masters, who in turn beat them savagely. The Dissenting Academies were a great contrast and expected boys to be almost too well behaved, while the subjects taught were more up-to-date. Dr. Priestley, the scientist, taught at one of them.

Stubbs' horses are always painted with knowledge and affection, and here he has obviously also enjoyed doing the portraits of the high Curricle-Phaeton and its proud owners.

The wharf below London Bridge where the richest cargoes of all were unloaded. Here to the Old East India Wharf came bales of delicate silks, chests packed with Chinese porcelain, and carvings and aromatic spices and coffee from India and the South Seas.

It was during this century that the city of Bath became the most celebrated and fashionable watering-place in England and, thanks to two architects, father and son, the elder of whom was generally known as Wood of Bath, one of the most civilized towns in the world. Bath has been, ever since Beau Nash, Wood, Alexander Pope, Congreve and Sheridan, very much a real city, elegantly urban, and yet small and never shutting out the soft green of the downs that surround it. The famous springs still run splendidly hot and have gently steamed ever since the Roman legionaries took their ease in the fine swimming-baths that their Italian engineers had designed (see pages 5-7).

Then after three hundred years, the Romans went home and for yet another three hundred years brambles twined,

foxes barked and birds nested among the roofless, crumbling ruins of the Roman pleasure city, while the hot springs were forgotten and, it is to be supposed, wasted themselves in sulphur-smelling marshes.

Monks came and built an Abbey and an Anglo-Saxon King was crowned in it, and, at long last, the great Roman baths and the hot springs were found again. Poor fat Queen Anne trundled down to Bath for her health. She may not have benefited much, but by her visit a new fashion was set, so that soon sharp gamesters and night-capped poets, old lords in their buckled shoes and with ribbons and stars gleaming on their embroidered coats, all came down to Bath in their coaches and chaises. Such ladies there were too! The old Duchess of Marlborough came, and the prettiest young

The City of Bath became the most celebrated, and fashionable watering-place in England. 'Beau Nash', the master of ceremonies at Bath, and the excellent Allen (who began by organizing posting horses and ended as the splendid owner of Prior Park) made it very much a little City, yet all so designed that its buildings never shut out the green of the downs and woods. These are photographs of its famous Crescent taken recently.

Bath has had a long history as a pleasure place, ever since the Romans discovered the hot springs, built a resort, and called it Aquae Sulis (the Waters of Sulis) after a local British god or possibly goddess.

At the time of Queen Anne's visit, when hoops were wide and wigs were prodigious, Bath itself had not yet arrived at its full beauty, for not even the architects and designers of Bath, not even 'Beau Nash', the 'King of Bath', or Allen

heiresses whose wide hoops held out their satin gowns and whose powdered curls made their pink-and-white complexions look even more delicious. All of them came to see or be seen, to drink the waters or to lose their hearts to a beau, or to squander a fortune at cards.

Over Bath there reigned for long the celebrated Beau Nash. He was the friend of Pope, of Addison, Steele and Congreve, and in general kept the best company. He, in his white cocked hat, was everywhere – in the Pump Room, or dancing at the subscription balls in the Assembly Rooms, or staking his money at the gaming tables, for he loved the sound of rattling dice and played high. But he was not just a gambler. He arranged that there should be fiddlers in the Pump Room in the morning and more fiddlers on the terraced walks, and he it was who for-

bade the wearing of swords anywhere in the city and who used to warn, pretty young, innocent belles and beaux against the many male and female fortune-hunters and card-sharpers.

By the time the picture they had planned was complete, by the time the scaffolding was fairly out of the way in the Crescent, the Circus, Pulteney Street, the New Assembly Rooms and all the rest, a new generation had begun coming to Bath; for the fashion for visits to Bath went on.

By 1800 a few of the young men would be in militia uniform, but that was all that was noticeable in Bath of the convulsions that were shaking Europe. The French Revolution was over, but the French were more of a danger than ever, with Napoleon always 'marching toward the sound of the cannon', as he said, stopping

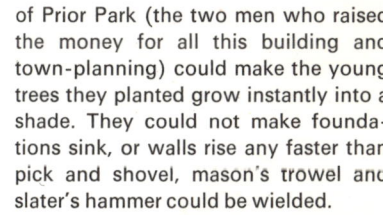

of Prior Park (the two men who raised the money for all this building and town-planning) could make the young trees they planted grow instantly into a shade. They could not make foundations sink, or walls rise any faster than pick and shovel, mason's trowel and slater's hammer could be wielded.

By the time Bath was the place pictured here, there were new fashions in the shop-windows and in the heads of the young ladies. Now the girls wore low-necked dresses made of sprigged muslin – long, narrow-skirted, high-waisted – worn with the sweetest bonnets. The new generation of young men looked different too as they ogled some pretty creature coming out of the Pump Room, or spanking along in their light, elegant gigs down Pulteney Street, their varnished wheels glinting in the sun. Most of the young men were dressed as the picture shows – just a few would be in militia uniform.

'The moon was mounting up the sky and nowhere did abide'
1780–1810

Mow Cop, in Staffordshire, was built on purpose as a ruin. The new fashion was for 'the picturesque'. Poetry too was following the same trend.

The poet Byron looked not to the past but abroad to contemporary Greece, or into his own stormy heart.

Shelley's lyrical spirit looked to human love, and the love of freedom.

Keats looked to the visible world of nature.

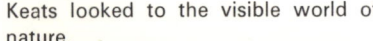

Wordsworth, below, was one of the greatest of the Lake poets.

our trade, crowning himself Emperor, striking out, now east, now west, with the kingdoms toppling. There were no more 'grand tours' for the rich young men, for Napoleon was blockading Britain. But this of course all helped Bath.

And yet it was novels about ruined abbeys and the ghosts of unfortunate damsels, or of prowling Italian bandits, that the pretty girls found so thrilling and for which the flowered bonnets could be seen bobbing off to the circulating library. As today, younger readers then liked their novels and romances to be as bloodstained as possible with perhaps rather more tombstones, midnight yells, daggers, and clanking chains than would be fashionable now. In *Northanger Abbey*, Jane Austen's charming little goose of a heroine, Catherine Morland, says that she hears 'that something very shocking will soon come out in London; it will be uncommonly dreadful; more horrible than anything we have met with yet!'

Those novels were often as absurd as our horror-films. They were the 'pop' version of a change in taste that set free some of the best poets and painters that Britain has ever had. The change to 'the romantic' can be seen in the pictures of artists such as the group now called 'the Norwich School' or in Morland and Turner, and in the poems of writers such as Shelley, Keats, Byron and Sir Walter Scott, as well as those of a group who became known as the 'Lake Poets'. Dr Johnson's stately prose, Pope's measured verse, Gainsborough's gentlefolk in stately parks, had begun to seem stiff and boring.

Readers had begun to be thrilled by mediaeval times, painters to love country scenes. The taste was for mountains, waterfalls and forests. Poets wrote 'singing lines' that have never been forgotten about simple country things:

> 'My Luve is like a red, red rose,
> That's newly sprung in June:
> My Luve is like the melodie,
> That's sweetly play'd in tune'

wrote Robert Burns, the Scottish ploughman-poet. Burns and Shelley were among

Steam!

those who, like Byron, were actively left-wing in politics.

Wordsworth and Coleridge among the Lake Poets – less political – tried consciously to get rid of long words. *The Ancient Mariner* and *Kubla Khan* seem to the present writer to be, to this day, 'compulsive' reading – wild, magical, haunting, mysterious. Coleridge's poems are famous – what is not perhaps so well known is that the lectures of one of the leading scientists of the day, Humphry Davy, given at the Royal Institution, were often attended by this leader among the romantic poets. Coleridge would go because, he said, Davy's eloquence gave him fresh ideas:

'Chemistry is not only a matter of minute experiments with crucibles, but [is concerned] with the great forms and elements of the whole world – sunshine, winds, clouds, rivers and cataracts – and the scene of their operations in the face of nature itself – the sky, mountains, plains and valleys. The superiority of modern over ancient times is connected with our knowledge of the [natural] world. Men of science have examined with reverence and awe the substantial majesty of nature.'

At the Royal Institution was also Humphry Davy's marvellous pupil, the young Faraday who became one of the greatest as well as the most charming of experimental scientists.

Naturally some people thought both the new simplicity and the new wildness just as shocking or as funny as older people today think 'modern' painting and modern fiction. A lot of amusement was got by younger verse-writers by parodying both old and new.

It so happened that Drury Lane Theatre was burned down (in 1771) and under pretence that all the leading poets had competed in writing verses to be said at the opening of the rebuilt theatre, two brothers, James and Horace Smith, parodied them all. One of the poets parodied is supposed to be a pompous patriot who blames every sort of thing that had ever gone wrong, including of course the Drury Lane fire, on 'the Corsican Upstart', the Monster, Buonaparté (Napoleon hated his name to be spelt like that).

Steam hadn't got to fairs yet but there were 'Roundabouts'. Notice the coach.

'Who makes the price of dry goods and
   tobaccos?
Who makes the quartern loaf and Luddites
   rise?
Who fills the butchers' shops with large
   blue flies?'
                  'Tis Bony!'

The reader has to imagine what even the most advanced countries had been like up to now. With two notable exceptions, 'work' and 'production', that is, to say, the ploughing and digging, the spinning and weaving, and the getting people and goods from place to place, had all been done by the power of human and animal muscles. The exceptions were that ships had *sailed* – that is, used the power of wind – while corn had been ground and water pumped either by wind power or water power. The new devices whose pictures are shown here– the machines for spinning and then for weaving – were at first worked by an old power, the force of running water. This is why the first textile factories – Lancashire cotton-mills and later the Yorkshire woollen–mills – were all built in valleys where the force of a running stream would set the new devices in movement. But just before this time a new revolutionary use for water had been found. What is striking is that it was used and applied, not just by one inventor in one place, but by several men in several places.

First came Savery's original, unsatisfactory power unit (see page 90); then Newcomen in 1717 with the Engine for

Watt from Scotland, while working with Boulton from the Midlands, greatly improved the steam-engine.

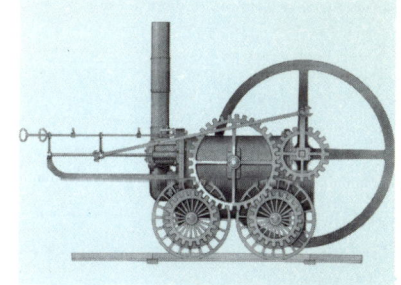

Trevithick, the Cornish mine-captain, improved a high-pressure pumping engine and put it on wheels. It became a locomotive. It weighed 5 tons and would pull a load of thirty tons at 5 miles per hour, but at first he had not been sure that any engine could haul itself. So, one dark night, he hired a chaise but no horse and he and a confidential friend moved it along by turning the wheels by hand. Notice the cogs.

'Puffing Billy'. Most early locomotives have perished but the famous Puffing Billy, after about 50 years continuous pulling and hauling on Tyneside, is now in honourable retirement in the Science Museum. 'Billy' was designed in 1813 by William Hedley.

James Hargreaves named his celebrated 'Spinning Jenny' after his wife.

Raising Water with a Power made by Fire' (see page 114), a great improvement.

What these two and others pioneered was nothing less than the large-scale use of the immense natural force of the expansion into steam of heated water. James Watt from Clydeside applied the force more cunningly; Trevithick, from the tin mines of Cornwall, put his steam engine on wheels and the resulting 'steam carriage' on roads whose surfaces were too hopelessly bad. Stephenson, from Newcastle, made a really practical 'railway locomotive'. It was proved that a steam locomotive could pull a heavy 'train' of coaches and waggons. But in fact the world had not got just a fine new great pump, or a superb pulling device, but 'Power'.

Steam power could work looms, turn spinning-wheels, plough, thresh, and, in a dozen ways, do the work of men's, women's and horses' muscles. It was as yet only down in dark mines or in grimy sheds in Northern England and the Scottish Lowlands, that the still clumsy bringers of a new age coughed, clattered and thumped out the pattern of the future. Proud, heavy Shire horses, or tugging yokes of oxen, still ploughed or

dragged great loads. Light pack-ponies still trotted inland from the fishing ports with fresh oysters or whitebait, for the Mayor's or the Squire's table, or with smuggled French lace or brandy. Smart young men in Bath still took pretty young ladies out driving in gleaming gigs. But in fact a time of quick change had begun.

What sort of change? Clubs and societies began to spring up to discuss the new inventions. Some of them were rather like descendants of the Royal Society which had fallen, temporarily, into a paralytic state. The Lunar Society in Birmingham met on nights when there was a moon by whose light to ride home. Here Watt, and that jolly iron-founder Boulton, and Erasmus Darwin the biologist-poet, debated and joked. Then there was the Manchester Philosophical Society with Dalton, the man who listed the elements. There were also less clubbable inventors – that hot-tempered Cornishman Trevithick, for instance. Many of these scientists and inventors felt passionately about politics, favoured the French Revolution, but hated Napoleon. Things went wrong, for the great technical changes were not really understood, even by people who made the inventions. Two Revolutions – political and industrial – happening together meant confusion as well as callousness. In the north of England, especially, thousands of working-class families suffered hardship and despair because of unconsidered, unshock-absorbed, jolting change. The Luddites rose and destroyed the machines that had robbed them of their jobs, and so did the 'Rebecca men (against the charges at the toll-gates on the public roads). There was no 'welfare state'. Great fortunes were soon to be made, most people were slightly better off, but some were desperate. Their violence led in turn to vicious hitting back.

As the tale goes on (and right into our own times) the reader will very likely decide that forethought and cushioning against jolts ought to be used whenever new technical devices get under way and change for the better begins. The cottagers whose common rights the enclosures swallowed, the displaced handloom-weavers, and later the miners, male and female, together with their wretched children all suffered at this time, yet England as a whole prospered.

We began this part of the tale with the words of a free-spoken French citizen who, because he spoke his mind, didn't get on with his own government. Many years later another French citizen, who also didn't get on with a different French government, had things to say about Britain. This time the traveller was a woman, Madame de Staël. When she came to England, Napoleon, whom she loathed, had not yet been completely defeated, but she understood politics and felt sure that his end was in sight.

She knew all the great people of her day, for she was the daughter of the financier Necker, who had tried in vain to put the French government's economy to rights, just before the French Revolution. Napoleon hated Madame de Staël as much as she hated him. It seems odd that an Emperor should have hated a private citizen so much and for so long. But she was clever and rich, and a writer whose books were read and she had many friends. As Napoleon's Empire swallowed up one European country after another, Madame de Staël kept moving. From Switzerland she travelled to Sweden and thence to England, and was received as a great 'lion' (the current name for a V.I.P., a star, a celebrity). Everyone wanted to meet the woman who stood up to the Emperor and to hear the latest news from the Continent. One evening in 1813 she met Lord Byron, Lord Lansdowne, Mr Whitbread, Sir Humphry Davy, Lady Davy, and a great many other celebrated people at a dinner party at Holland House. Byron wrote his impressions; 'She was vain, but who had an excuse for vanity if she had not?' She seemed greatly impressed at the excellent state in which she found things here. Britain seemed to be by no means ruined by the long war and Napoleon's blockade. The population was on its way up, from nine to fourteen millions, and the country was richer, not poorer. Why? Was it thanks to William Pitt our great Prime

Minister? Nelson? Wellington? She thought not. She wrote:

'For all this, England owes far less thanks to the results of its policy and the success of its Army and Navy, than to the inventions of men like Watt, Davy, Hargreaves, Crompton, Arkwright and Cartwright, by whom the territory of commerce and industry has been peacefully overcome and who by means of coal, iron and steel have revolutionized the world.'

She only instances one scientist, Davy; the others are technicians.

Two years after that dinner-party, in 1815, Napoleon escaped from the island of Elba, to which he had been exiled after defeats in 1813 and 1814. Once out, he began once more to terrorize Europe. For a hundred days he was free and in this time he gathered an army and the Allies gathered their troops against him. The final battle was fought at Waterloo. The general in charge of the Allied forces was the Duke of Wellington. It was a great victory for the Allies, Napoleon was exiled again, and after it was all over, Wellington, having ridden round the corpse-stricken battlefield, wrote a celebrated sentence: 'Nothing except a battle lost can be half as melancholy as a battle won'.

The Duke of Wellington was commanding our armies in the Peninsular War when Goya, that perceptive Spanish painter, made this likeness. Goya hated war. It was the Duke's profession, and yet . . . ! (see in the text what he said about his greatest victory).

Tyrant or liberator? Napoleon Bonaparte, the corporal who made himself Emperor – the best loved, most hated, and most capable man of his age. He only lacked 'humility and a human heart.'

Evidence, gaps and survivals.

1714–1815

Senior Gatekeeper, Bank of England.

Nelson's Column, Trafalgar Square.

EVIDENCE

The text will already have suggested to the reader that there are a great many very rich written sources – novels, plays, parodies, epic poems, biographies and memories. Then there are histories, pamphlets and political orations written sometimes by Whigs and sometimes by Tories. These give splendidly lop-sided views of what really happened, for they were by men who had taken an active part in politics, partisans who praised their friends and lashed any other party. Today political historians pick a careful way between contradictory statements.

The various debating clubs, such as the Lunar Society and the august (but towards the later part of the time, rather sleepy) Royal Society, all kept records, while manuals on shop-keeping and shop-keepers' ledgers often survive. The great voyages such as those of Captain Cook may be recorded not only in the official ships' logs but by the scientists on board. There were famous trials too – those of Warren Hastings (India) and of George IV's Queen Caroline for example.

Most 'By-gones' in Folk Museums date from this time and elegant clothes – both men's and women's – have been preserved. In fact it is possible to know a very great deal about all the prosperous inhabitants of both England and Scotland.

GAPS

But we do not know for certain why so many of the children even of prosperous

The Royal State Coach, completed in 1761 and used at coronations.

people died, and when it comes to finding out what has happened to the less prosperous – that is of course to the great majority – there are a great many gaps. There are crude statistics, but this question of infant mortality for instance – deaths of children under five – was it usually due to infectious disease, poverty, or perhaps the wrong food? A mixture no doubt, but in what proportion?

Then there were practically no school registers, so historians have only vague ideas as to who got how many years schooling. And, though many schools were both stupid and brutal, some (the Quaker schools for instance) seem to have been pretty good. It would be interesting to know what percentage of the population could read and write at the time when Voltaire looked at England in the early 1700s, and then again when Madame de Staël came in the early 1800s. Pretty certainly more girls and women were illiterate than boys and men.

SURVIVALS

Much furniture, silver and china dating from this century are of course still in daily use, while as for buildings, the City of Bath and whole streets of other towns remain.

Today sailor's uniforms are said to recall Admiral Lord Nelson and his victories. A 'sailor collar' is edged with three rows of tape, which are said to be: one for Cape St Vincent, one for Copenhagen, and the third for Trafalgar, while the soft black tie was first worn as mourning for the Navy's best-loved Admiral.

The reader will also doubtless call to mind a certain famous London square and a well-known London railway station in whose names survive two famous battles.

There are also a number of technical or semi-technical words in common use that were invented or brought into use at this time. 'Horse power' is one, 'navvy' is another. Various kinds of immunization of today are often called 'vaccination' after Jenner's cowpox discovery, and there are also a number of words as well as concepts used by electricians that go back to the inventors, Faraday, Ampère, Volta and Galvani.

FOREWORD TO TEXTS AND COMMENTS

This short supplement will be, its author hopes, not only interesting to individual readers, but of special use in schools for group or class project work.

The information in it is of three kinds:

(1) Additional background about everyday life.

(2) More about the lives of interesting individuals and historical oddities.

(3) Samples from contemporary novels, or biographies and gossip, or from what research historians have to say.

What has been included in it is meant as an appetizer. The hope is that readers' curiosity will be encouraged and that they will get an idea of how many rich sources there are. A short annotated book list has also been included on page vi.

FOLLOWING UP

In choosing what to follow up after reading any history, it is usually best to be guided first by inclination and then by what lies to hand.

The story of a particular place (small for choice) or of a particular class of thing – furniture-making, glass-blowing, the building of lighthouses, or the digging of canals – is usually far more entertaining and enlightening than a national history, though a general outline on which to build is just as necessary as it is for a mammal to have a skeleton. Just to follow the changing story of food and meals, coal-mining, the making of pottery or the fashions in dress, can be more enthralling than to study the history of a nation. To read the history of one particular place can be startling. Perhaps it turns out to be tragic with battles, plagues and witch-burnings, or comic with odd characters such as 'Old Parr', or the Vicar of Bray, or – like Richmond Hill or Sherwood Forest – charming with songs and ballads.

Best of all is perhaps to uncover the tale of some man or woman who, unknown or scarcely known, yet, in his or her day, added something real to knowledge, to the arts, to happiness or to health. Such characters crop up not only in every place but in the tale of every invention, science and art, from that of growing turnips to that of teaching children. Another often startling experience can be to read of some international event as it is recorded in, say, a French, American or Irish history.

Reading is of course far from being the only (or even perhaps the best) way of following up some special historical interest.

Great houses and the manifold things in them, the farming or manufacturing 'bygones' now often collected in museums hold clues that set the imagination to work. There are many new special museums or special displays in older museums. To instance only two: one, the Wedgwood Museum (Barlaston, Stoke-on-Trent) not only tells the story of England's most famous pottery but is full of vivid little portrait-medallions done at the time, of celebrities such as Captain Cook or Nelson. A second instance is the Waterways Museum (at Stoke Bruerne, near Towcester in Northamptonshire). Here, writes the curator, may be seen 'legging boards' on which boatmen lay to push their boats through tunnels; traditional clothing and a full-size reconstruction of a butty boat-cabin fitted out and decorated in the traditional way.

To see things, to discover some 'bygone', is to bring the written word to life. Something however was said by the great French scientist, Louis Pasteur, that is as true of history as of science: 'Chance favours the mind that is prepared.' The thing chanced upon in a museum, in a friend's attic or on a holiday, will always be blank to the finder who comes upon it with a blank mind.

Texts and comments

page

97, Voltaire
98
Voltaire was later the guest of Frederick the Great, King of Prussia. He wrote a celebrated letter home. Each sentence begins with praise and ends with 'but ...'. Something like this:

'The King's supper parties are delightful; but ...'

'I have been given a splendid set of apartments; but ...'.

In England he had fine things to say; but .... One 'but' was that, though they were handsome, the great ladies of London were badly educated and consequently stupid compared with those of Paris.

99 What the young Halley had done
Edmund Halley was the young man who had persuaded the great moody Sir Isaac Newton not to keep to himself his mathematical proofs of what had been observed by Kepler and Galileo. Professor Andrade, writing recently, says, 'Sir Isaac Newton was one of the greatest men in the history of human thought'. Yet if the cheerful and unselfish Halley had not persuaded him, Newton's greatest work might never have been known.

100, The Eddystone Reef
101
The danger to be marked was (and is) a pair of rocks, only visible at low tide, that form the crest of a long reef that rises out of deep water, south – west from Plymouth harbour. At high water nothing but the bursting of breakers is to be seen.

'For ten or fourteen days together the sea would be so raging about these rocks (caused by outwinds and the running of the ground-seas) that although the weather should be calm in other places, yet here it would mount and fly more than 200 feet.'

103 Tartans and 'the '45'
In common with most governments that have had a fright, the English Government now behaved badly and stupidly. They forbade Clansmen to wear the primitive Highland dress of the day. Mr. McBain wrote:

'The old Highland dress was a saffron shirt, a plaid (10 yards long) thrown over the shoulder and brought down to the knees all round in pleats and then belted, a bonnet (sometimes), and brogues made of skin (sometimes with hose); knees always bare. The modern kilt is merely the lower half of the plaid cut off from the upper.'

Highlandmen used to sleep in the plaid and 'put it into a kilt' when they got up.

The Celebrated Vicar of Bray
The ballad is famous, and new, satiric versions of it are often circulated. The original story goes back to the time of Henry VIII. See page 47, in the companion volume *Tudor England*.

'The vivacious Vicar of Bray living under King Henry VIII, King Edward VI, Queen Mary I, and Queen Elizabeth I, was first a Catholic, then a Protestant, then a Catholic, then a Protestant again. He had seen some martyrs burnt (two miles off) at Windsor, and found this fire too hot for his tender temper.' This vicar was taxed by one for being a turncoat. 'Not so' said he, 'for I always kept my principle, which is this – to live and die the Vicar of Bray.'

In the time of George I a young officer wrote a ballad that immediately became famous:

'In good King Charles's golden days,
 When loyalty had no harm in 't,
A zealous High Churchman I was,
 And so I got preferment.
To teach my flock I never miss'd
 Kings were by God appointed,
And they are damned who dare resist,
 Or touch the Lord's anointed.

CHORUS 'And this is law I will maintain,
 Until my dying day, Sir,
That whatsoever King shall reign,
 I'll still be the Vicar of Bray, Sir.'

Then this cheerful officer takes the tale into his own times and continues about suiting oneself to whichever party is in power – Whigs or Tories, Hanoverians, Jacobites, Catholics, Protestants. In James II's reign he is sure that a man who wants to get on in the world will find that the Church of Rome suits very nicely; in the time of William and Mary he will become deeply Protestant – a Tory, but still a Protestant. In Queen Anne's time, and in the time of George I (which for some reason he calls 'pudding time') he had better become a staunch Whig and 'almost every day abjure the Pope and the Pretender'.

104, Comic Verse about the New Agriculture
105,
106
A sarcastic set of verses was written anonymously about those prize rams, *A Satirical poem addressed to the Norfolk Agricultural Society*:

'And why poor harmless sheep oppress
With such enormous loads of grease?
Nor follow such expensive plans
For deluging of dripping pans?
Alas! What tantalizing meat,
Too dear to buy, too fat to eat! ...
All is so level, smooth and sleek
For legs, head, tail in vain you seek.
What do you see that man can swallow?
One narrow stripe twixt bone and tallow.'

And so on with more verses of baleful derision.

Arthur Young and Agriculture in France
Arthur Young before he became a successful writer was an unsuccessful farmer. He rode about, both in England and on the Continent, to see what was being done and wrote books about the new methods. In France no one as yet seems to have been doing anything about this 'New Agriculture'. This may well have been because French laws and especially the way farms were taxed were bad. Voltaire had already written about the contrast:

'The feet of the peasants in England are not bruised with wearing wooden shoes; they eat white bread, are well clothed, and are not afraid of increasing their plots nor of putting tiles instead of thatch on their houses, for fear that their taxes will be raised the year following.'

Voltaire is writing about the French 'taille', a bitterly resented way of taxing. To make improvements on a farm in France would mean paying more to the tax-collector.

'Cursed and Disgraceful Roads'
In England there were other, but lesser, obstacles to improvement. Young travelled long distances and swears at the horrible state of the roads.

Of all the cursed roads that ever disgraced this kingdom in the very ages of barbarism, none ever equalled that from Billericay to the King's Head at Tilbury. It is for near twelve miles so narrow that a mouse cannot pass by any carriage. I saw a fellow creep under his waggon to assist me to lift, if possible, my chaise over a hedge. To add to all the infamous circumstances which concur to plague a traveller, I must not forget the eternally meeting with chalk waggons, themselves frequently stuck fast, till a collection of them are in the same situation. Twenty or thirty horses may be tacked to each to draw them out one by one!'

106, Shop Signs are necessary before people can read
107
It seems that by the 18th century, the ordinary shop-signs more or less like the inn-signs of today, had developed.

x

Dorothy Davis, in her delightful *History of Shopping*, writes:

'Enormous, carved, gilded and painted symbols hung out over the streets, and in narrow thoroughfares met overhead. Some were so monstrously heavy that they pulled out the house-fronts, and several fell down and injured passers-by. By mid-century, public opinion was demanding some sort of control. The signs were very large, very fine, and very absurd, golden periwigs, saws, axes, lancets, razors, trees, knives, salmon, cheeses, blacks' heads, half-moons, sugar loaves and Westphalian hams. Their splendid profusion of colours and shapes had become the most conspicuous feature of the city streets; they had dripped on rainy days and creaked on windy nights for as long as anyone could remember and in 1762 they still clustered overhead in their thousands, more elaborate than ever before. Then they were suddenly removed in one clean sweep by order of the authorities.'

107 The Grand Tour

Young men of good family commonly were sent on tours of Europe. Accounts of such tours often sound splendid, so it is startling to read this, by James Boswell. (His *Life of Dr. Johnson* is famous.) This was in Hanover in the middle of the usual feasting with Royal Dukes, and Court Balls:

Thus was I laid. In the middle of a great room, upon straw spread on the floor. On the straw was a sheet; I had another sheet as a coverlet. On one side of me were eight or ten horses; on the other, four or five cows. A little way from me sat on high a cock and many hens; and before I went to sleep the cock made my ears ring with his shrill voice. What frightened me not a little was an immense mastiff chained pretty near the head of my bed. He growled most horribly, and rattled his chain. I called for a piece of bread and made a friendship with him. Before me were two great folding doors wide open, so that I could see the beauties of the evening sky. In this way, however, did I sleep with much contentment, and much health.

Dr. Johnson

The great Dr. Johnson was one of Garrick's great friends and was as famous for the amusing things he said as for his great dictionary, his poems, and his then popular tales and essays. Here are a few samples of the sort of things he said and that his friends (especially James Boswell and Mrs. Thrale) wrote down.

ON THE FAMILY INCOME

'Sir, no money is better spent than what is laid out for domestic satisfaction. A man is pleased that his wife is drest as well as other people; and a wife is pleased that she is drest.'

ON FOOLISH THINKING

'My dear friend, clear your mind of cant! You may say to a man, 'Sir, I am your most obedient, humble servant.' You are *not* his most obedient, humble servant! You may say, 'These are bad times; it is a melancholy thing to be reserved to such times.' You don't mind the times! You tell a man, 'I am sorry you had such bad weather the last day of your journey.' You don't care sixpence whether he is wet or dry. You may *talk* in this manner; it is a mode of talking in Society: but don't *think* foolishly.'

ON SAILORS

'No man will be a sailor who has contrivance enough to get himself into a jail; for being in a ship is being in a jail, with the chance of being drowned. A man in a jail has more room, better food, and commonly better company.'

ON 'GLORIOUS WAR'

'A fire might as well be thought a good thing as a war – there is the bravery of the firemen employed in extinguishing it. There is much humanity exerted in saving the lives and properties of the poor sufferers. Yet after all this who can say a fire is a good thing?'

'Of the thousands and ten thousands that perished in our late contests with France and Spain, most never felt the stroke of an enemy, but languished in tents and ships and died of fevers – pale, torpid, spiritless, and helpless; gasping and groaning . . . and were at last whelmed in pits or heaved into the ocean, without notice and without remembrance.'

DO AS I SAY AND NOT AS I DO

'No man practises so well as he writes. I have, all my life long, been lying in bed till noon; yet I tell all young men, and tell them with great sincerity, that nobody who does not rise early will ever do any good.'

107 Meals

Mr. Arnold Palmer in his *Moveable Feasts* reports:

'A Swiss pastor, C. P. Moritz, who spent a holiday in England in 1782, was given no more than tea and bread-and-butter for his breakfast. "The slices of bread and butter which they give you with your tea are thin as poppy leaves. But there is another kind of bread and butter usually eaten with tea, which is toasted by the fire and is incomparably good. This is called toast".'

108, 109 Some Dangers involved in being a Civil Engineer (The Voyage of the Neptune back to Port)

'Mr. Smeaton, hearing a sudden alarm and clamour overhead, ran up on deck in his shirt'.

It was dark, raining hard, and blowing. 'The first thing I saw', says Smeaton, 'was the horrible appearance of breakers; one of the seamen crying out, 'For God's sake, heave hard at that rope!' I laid hold and hauled with all my strength.'

The jibsail was blown to pieces, and, to save the mainsail, it was lowered, when fortunately the vessel obeyed her helm and rounded off. The sailors did not know at what part of the coast they were. At daybreak they found themselves out of sight of land, and the vessel driving towards the Bay of Biscay.

Another night and day passed. Finally, after having been thus blown about at sea for four days, they came to an anchor in Plymouth Sound.

Lighthouse Keepers

Smeaton was often anxious. After a storm his lighthouse keeper reports:

'The house did shake as if a man had been in a great tree, the men were almost frightened out of their lives. The fear seized them in the back, but rubbing them with oil of turpentine gave them relief.'

'The stone lighthouses of today' (so Trinity House now reports) 'still shake in violent storms, and pictures are sometimes thrown off the walls.'

'Smeaton's lighthouse stood for 120 years, the light itself being gradually improved. The 24 candles were, in 1810, replaced by 24 oil-lamps with reflectors behind them; then, in 1845, a dioptric or refracting lens with a single light in the centre was substituted, much as at the present day.'

109 Cook's Voyages

'Young Nick's Point', a high headland on the north-west coast of New Zealand, was named by Captain Cook after one of his ship's boys who had spied land from the masthead.

Captain Cook was shocked to find that the Maoris were cannibals. Why were they?

Always interested in diet, he thought it might be because there were (and are) no native mammals in New Zealand, and that Maoris suffered from what is known to-day as 'protein deficiency'. The story goes that, on his second and third voyages, he brought sows and boars which he let loose in pairs on both islands. Today, pigs that have gone wild are destructive of native bush. They are rough-looking creatures, thin and long-legged. Pig-hunting is necessary to keep down their numbers. Such pigs are popularly called 'Captain Cookers'.

The Scientific Side

Sir Joseph Banks (1740 – 1820) was already a well known botanist. In Cook's *Endeavour*, Banks and his team of scientists went west to South America, round Cape Horn to Australia, then on to New Zealand. Then Captain Cook coasted and charted (dangerously) inside the Great Barrier Reef and so to New Guinea, and on to the Cape of Good Hope, and so home.

Endeavour's scientists became famous. Every learned society in Europe put Banks' name on its list of honorary members and he was elected president of the Royal Society. He was a fearless man and he, Cook and Dr. Solander were particularly good both with timid, and threatening, tribesmen.

111 Why Canals?

The shocking state of the roads (see Texts and Comments ref. page 86) made it urgent to find a way of getting heavy goods to the customers. The great changes of the 'Industrial Revolution' would have been impossible with only these poor roads and coasting ships. Canals, and later the railways, have been called the arteries of the Industrial Revolution.

Canal travel, however, was slow, but by 1805 to 1830 in the great days of the stage-coach (see De Quincey's description on page 118) a new kind of road had been engineered on which express coaches could run. These new roads had mostly been made and taken over by 'Turnpike Companies' who charged tolls (see page 118).

112

The Emperor of China, unlike the Great Mogul, felt perfectly secure. When in 1792 a British emissary, Lord Macartney, brought him a polite letter from his fellow-ruler George III along with the customary present, the Emperor wrote back in words which could hardly have been more haughty:

'We have perused your memorial, O King, which reveals a devout humility. In consideration of his long journey we have shown your emissary special favour.

Swaying the wide world, we are not deflected by gifts. If we have commanded that your tribute offerings are to be accepted, it was not because we have any interest in outlandish objects, but solely in consideration for the proper spirit which prompted you to dispatch them from your remote island. We are in need of nothing, we possess all things. It is now your duty, King, to display in the future an even greater devotion than has inspired you in the past, by perpetual submission to the Dragon Throne.'

113 Justices of the Peace

Fielding, the excellent novelist who wrote *Tom Jones*, became a Justice of the Peace for Westminster. This was about twenty years after *The Beggar's Opera* was first produced. A recent writer, Mr. Hesketh Pearson, explains:

'The justices received no salaries and the Westminster ones made what they could from the prisoners brought before them. Most were worse than the thieves they condemned. They accepted bribes from the wealthy and encouraged the arrest of as many people as possible so that they could pocket the fees for releasing them on bail. They were known as 'Trading Justices' and were universally despised.'

Fielding quickly put an end to such a shocking state of things. He says that he did this by composing instead of inflaming the quarrels of porters and beggars and by refusing to take a shilling from a man who most undoubtedly would

not have had another left. Fielding reduced an income of about £500 a year 'of the dirtiest money on earth' to little more than £300, a considerable portion of which remained with his clerk:

'Indeed if the whole had gone to the clerk he would have been but ill-paid for sitting almost sixteen hours in the twenty-four in the most unwholesome, nauseous air in the universe which hath in his case corrupted a good constitution without contaminating his morals.'

114 Blots and Failures

Dr. John Hunter (brother to Jenner's teacher) used to remark that the art of surgery would not advance until professional men had the courage to publish their failures as well as their successes. Watt, the engineer, said the thing most wanted in mechanical engineering was a history of failures: 'We want,' he said, 'a book of blots.' Sir Humphry Davy said: 'I thank God I was not made a dexterous manipulator, for the most important of my discoveries have been suggested to me by failures.'

117 The Rights of Man

The French 'Declaration of the Rights of Man' in 1793 included three very important rights. The Right to Social Assistance (Welfare), the Right to Free Education, and the Right to Work.

The Declaration of 1789 had not been nearly so plain and far-reaching and, says J. G. Talman, a present-day historian, it seems to have been drafted by comfortably-off people 'who lived in no fear of unemployment, poverty or disease', or of being unable to get an education for their children.

Many historians now think of the first part of the French Revolution as being mainly a middle-class revolt.

The Seamen cannot stand it

The picture at the bottom of page 117 concerns the celebrated naval mutiny of Spithead and the Nore (1797). For several years pitiful letters had been sent to the Lords of the Admiralty by the men before the mast:

'We don't wish to go to sea in H.M.S. Winchelsea. Our usuage was more like Turks than of British seamen. We are noct about so that we do not no what to do. Every man in her would sooner be shot at like a taregaite by muskettree than remain any longer in her.'

On H.M.S. *Shannon*, lying at Sheerness, the men complained of:

'the ill-treatment which we have and do receve from the tiriant of a Captain, which is more than the spirits and harts of true English Men can clearly bear, for we are born free but now we are slaves.'

In the book from which these extracts are taken (*The Floating Republic* by G. E. Manwaring and B. Dobree) there is an account of something that amounted almost to murder.

'Three men were flogged without Court Martial, the punishment was inflicted with such horrible severity that they all three died in less than twenty-four hours after it was over.'

While the mutiny was on and while the mutineers had complete control of the fleet no officer was attacked.

124 The Clergyman who invented a Power Loom

Edmund Cartwright, a clergyman, invented a power-loom in 1784. Lord Russell, the philosopher, told the present writer that Cartwright had at one time been tutor to his father.

'I doubt,' said Lord Russell, 'if my grandfather, who gave him the post, ever knew that he had invented anything. He was a suitable tutor because he knew Latin and was competent to construe the Odes of Horace.'

	English Politics	Foreign Affairs, Exploration, Colonies, Trade	Literature, Architecture, Painting, Music	Science & Technics — Europe and America	Science & Technics — Britain
1720 to 1740	*Hanoverian Succession* George I (1714-1727) South Sea Bubble Sir Robert Walpole P.M. Whig supremacy George II (1727-1760) Spain renounces Gibraltar Statutes against witchcraft repealed John Wesley, Methodist revival	French develop Mississippi as trading area The China trade Bering discovers Aleutian Islands Peter the Great (Russia) Louis XV (France) North and South Carolina (crown colonies)	*Robinson Crusoe*, Defoe Voltaire, French writer *Gulliver's Travels*, Swift *Beggar's Opera* Gay Bach, German composer *Rule Britannia* first sung Alexander Pope, poet Richardson, novelist	Linnaeus, Swedish botanist Buffon, French zoologist Rubber first used in Europe	Guy's Hospital founded Kay's 'fly shuttle' James Watt (1736-1819), engineer
1740 to 1760	George II The '45'. Bonnie Prince Charlie (the Young Pretender) lands in Scotland from France. Gets down South as far as Derby Defeated at Culloden (April 1746) Seven Years War Elder Pitt becomes P.M.	University of Pennsylvania founded Clive in India Black hole of Calcutta Lisbon earthquake (20,000 dead) Elizabeth, Czarina of Russia French fight English in N. America and Canada Quebec, Wolfe	Handel's *Messiah* Hogarth's *Marriage a la Mode* Chardin, French painter Fielding's *Tom Jones* Rousseau, French philosopher Johnson's Dictionary Boswell and Paoli in Corsica Horace Walpole's sham-Gothick Strawberry Hill	Sugar extracted from beetroot Diderot and d'Alembert begin the French Encyclopaedia Franklin, American statesman, writer and scientist	Highway Act British Museum founded Calendar reform Bridgewater Canal First mine tramway Harrison's Chronometer
1760 to 1780	George III (1760-1820) 'Wilkes and Liberty' political agitation Lord North heads government of 'The King's Friends' Last attempt to prevent reporting of parliamentary debates Lord Mansfield decides slavery illegal in British Isles Edmund Burke, statesman and writer	Catherine the Great (Russia) Captain Cook sails 'Boston Tea Party' 'Continental Congress' meets in Philadelphia War of American Independence Burgoyne defeated at battle of Saratoga Declaration of Independence Convicts transported to Australia (instead of Virginia) Warren Hastings, 'Governor General' in India	Gluck, German composer Fragonard, French painter Laurence Sterne, novelist Reynolds, Gainsborough, English painters Haydn, Austrian composer Mozart, Austrian composer Sheridan, playwright Gibbon, historian Beaumarchais, *Barber of Seville* Adam Smith, economist	Galvani, Italian theories on electric current Mesmer, hypnotism Solander, Dutch naturalist	Hargreaves } spinning and Arkwright } weaving Priestley, chemistry of gases Cavendish, chemistry and physics J. Wedgwood, pottery Boulton and Watt, steam pumping engine
1780 to 1800	George III Gordon Riots Henry Grattan wants Home Rule for Ireland William Pitt the Younger becomes P.M. British seize French settlements in India, also Ceylon French fleet engages British in Channel Naval mutinies: Spithead and Nore	Louis XVI summons States General Dismisses Necker, his chief minister Storming of the Bastille (1789) Louis XVI attempts to leave France Trial and execution of Louis XVI Rise of Napoleon Napoleonic Wars begin City of Washington laid out; more states join original 13 Napoleon invades Egypt	Goethe, German poet Bentham, political philosopher Kant, German philosopher Schiller, German playwright Beethoven, German composer Burns, Scottish poet Blake, English poet Coleridge, English poet Tom Paine 'Rights of Man' Goya, Spanish painter	Laplace, French mathematician Whitney, American inventor of cotton gin Bougainville, French navigator Volta, Italian, electric science Lavoisier, French chemist	Herschel, discovery of Uranus Jenner, vaccination Malthus on population increase First 'Ordnance Survey' Lithography invented
1800 to 1815	George III Union of England and Ireland Resignation of Pitt, King disagrees with Catholic Emancipation Return of Pitt as P.M. Trafalgar Death of Pitt and Charles James Fox Prince of Wales becomes Regent Waterloo 1st census in Britain: Britain 10.4 million Ireland 5.2 million	Peace of Amiens (1802) Napoleon makes himself Emperor of France Blockade of Britain Napoleon invades Russia Triple Alliance against France Mungo Park (Africa) The War of 1812 against America The 100 Days Congress of Vienna (1815)	Wordsworth, English poet Turner, English painter Cobbett, English writer Walter Scott, Scottish novelist Jane Austen, English novelist Humboldt, German explorer naturalist Shelley, English poet Byron, English poet Keats, English poet	Pestalozzi, Italian educational reformer Lamarck, French zoologist Fulton, American, steam navigation	Telford, canals Gas for lighting Dalton, atomic table Davy, Miner's lamp John McAdam, roads and construction Lancaster } Mass Bell } education Robert Owen, social reformer Stephenson, *Rocket*

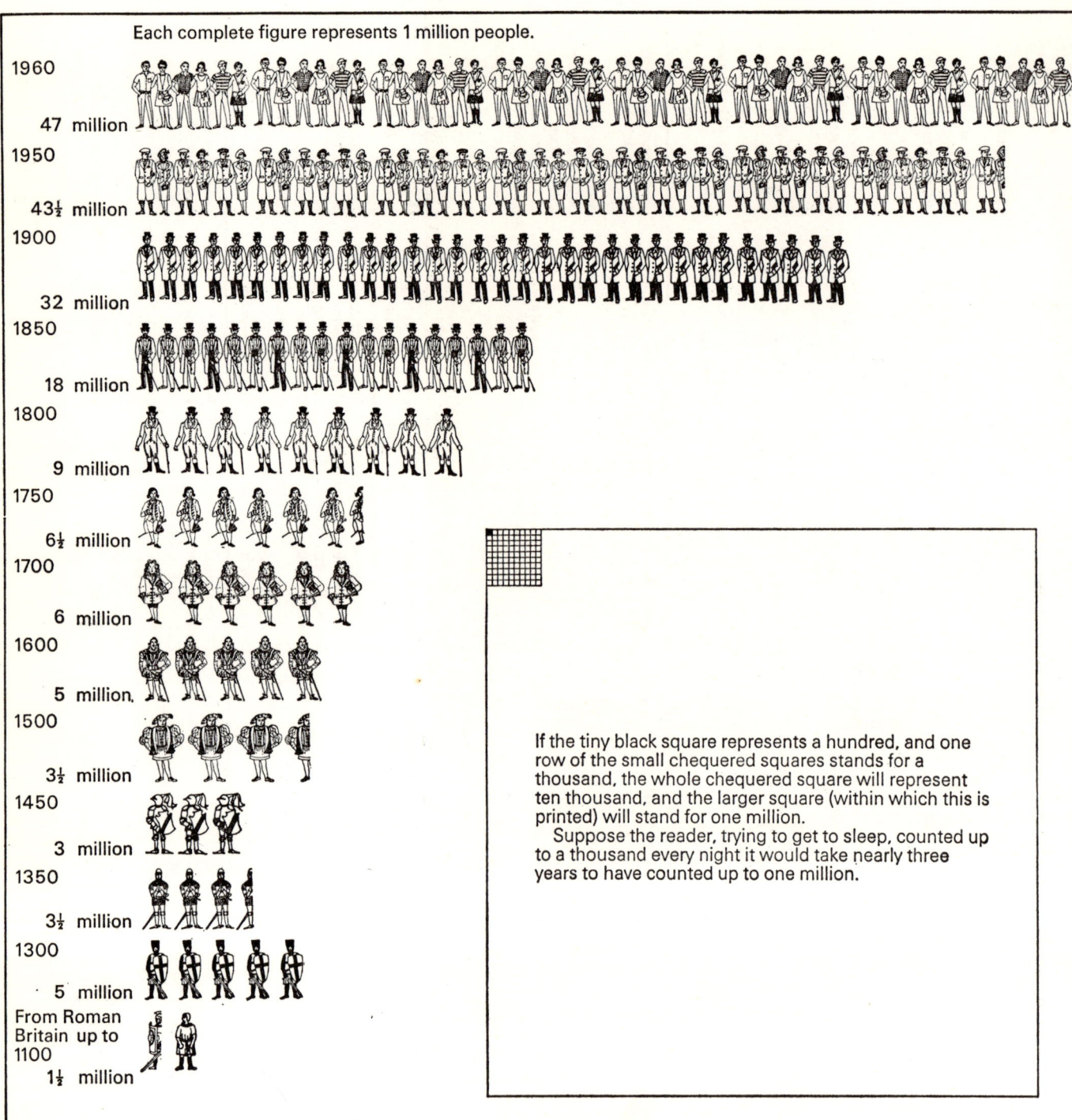

Each complete figure represents 1 million people.

1960	47 million
1950	43½ million
1900	32 million
1850	18 million
1800	9 million
1750	6½ million
1700	6 million
1600	5 million
1500	3½ million
1450	3 million
1350	3½ million
1300	5 million
From Roman Britain up to 1100	1½ million

If the tiny black square represents a hundred, and one row of the small chequered squares stands for a thousand, the whole chequered square will represent ten thousand, and the larger square (within which this is printed) will stand for one million.

Suppose the reader, trying to get to sleep, counted up to a thousand every night it would take nearly three years to have counted up to one million.

This population chart is very important not only for trying to make sense of English history, but because it suggests several puzzles. Up to 1801 (the first census) the figures are only estimates. But they are estimates to produce which all sorts of corroborating evidence and cunning checks and counterchecks have been used.

One hundred–million chart
It is genuinely difficult to grasp the difference between one big number and another, so that this little chart may surprise the reader. Yet in history, as in science, to be able to get some idea of 'orders of magnitude' helps the imagination.